THE GREAT DEPRESSION AND AMERICAN CAPITALISM

Problems in American Civilization

The Great DEPRESSION and AMERICAN CAPITALISM

EDITED WITH AN INTRODUCTION BY
Robert F. Himmelberg
FORDHAM UNIVERSITY

D. C. HEATH AND COMPANY · Boston
A division of RAYTHEON EDUCATION COMPANY

Library of Congress Catalog Card Number: 68-19013

INTRODUCTION

IN 1929 an unparalleled period in American economic history began which profoundly affected the nation's political and social development. Depressions had of course occurred many times before 1929. Like every other capitalist economy, America's has developed along a curve of forward surges alternating with more or less pronounced stretches of slow growth or retardation. But the cycle of business activity had never yet brought the economy to the depths it entered between 1929 and March 1933. At this latter point, with more than one fourth of the work force unemployed, with industrial production at half the 1929 level, the curve of business activity finally turned upward again.

But the years of upturn were in some respects more frightening than the years of descent. The recovery was weak and halting. Between 1933 and 1937 the economy's output grew at a painfully slow rate. In 1937 national income finally pulled abreast of the 1929 level, but eight million of a work force of forty million still remained unemployed. Worse, in the latter months of 1937 another downturn set in and again sent income and employment spiraling downward.

Though the downturn eased by mid-1938 and gave way to modest gains during 1939, it was not until defense spending mounted in 1940 and 1941 that the Great Depression was banished. The war period, 1942–1945, which strained the economy to previously unattained productive achievements seemingly ushered in a new era of economic expansion. In the two decades and more since the end of the war the business cycle has returned but with a demeanor much more modest

than it wore in the 1930's. Unemployment rates have stayed below the five percent mark except for limited periods during recessions, and the economy's total output had increased, by 1960, to well over twice its level in 1929.

What caused the Great Depression? Today the question has not quite the same urgency it had in the 1930's, but it remains important for anyone who wants to understand America's recent past and to speculate upon her future, for at least two reasons. The depression, in the first place, is a primary datum for the study of American economic history. It raises a number of questions that any meaningful discussion of the sources and pattern of American economic development, any appraisal of the economy's prospects for growth and stability, must take into account. Was the depression a unique event, an exception to the norm of successful economic performance? Or was it a revelation that the form of American capitalism prevailing until the 1930's, a form in which governmental influence upon economic decision-making was relatively limited, had exhausted its capacity to maintain satisfactory levels of prosperity? If the economy's performance has been good, or at least adequate, in the post-World War II period, should the fact be attributed to the economy's own resilience? Or should it be considered a result of the new governmental economic policies and institutions which were devised during the New Deal of the 1930's and which have been strengthened and extended since then? If this is the case, will it be possible to maintain governmental control over the economy at the prevailing level, or will that control have to be progressively enlarged until the areas of private decision-making shrink to insignificance?

The selections in this volume represent the major interpretive approaches of economists to the causes of the depression. These explanations offer material for fruitful consideration of these causes and other economic issues raised by the depression. Though the readings bear upon an economic problem and come from the pens of economists or commentators using the economist's tools, they also provide useful insights into recent American political history. The political history of the depression decade is largely the history of controversy over, and rapid change in, economic policy. Knowing the interpretations of the depression available to the political leaders of the '30's as a basis for policy formulation, a student can approach the politics of the period creatively. What economic considerations persuaded President Hoover to proceed so slowly and grudgingly (or so it seems today) in introducing innovations to combat the depression? What of the manifold changes in economic policy which came during Franklin D. Roosevelt's New Deal? Not all the measures of the Roosevelt era, it is true, were aimed simply at promoting recovery. Historians recently have suggested that many of the New Deal policies were simply the culmination of trends which might have reached fruition without the stimulus to social and economic reform created by the depression. Nevertheless many of the policies most characteristic of the New Deal were conceived primarily as recovery measures; the acid test for any proposal during the '30's was whether it appeared to promote a more prosperous economy. What interpretations of the depression did the New Dealers use to devise and justify their

proposals? How valid, upon reexamination, do these interpretations seem? In the light of interpretations available today but not fully available in the '30's, do we have any important reservations concerning the wisdom of some New Deal policies?

To present the material more clearly, and to illustrate the path of development that interpretive studies of the depression have taken, the readings are grouped into three categories. Each of these categories contains selections representing one of the three basic conceptual approaches to the depression since 1929.

Part I brings together explanations which share one of the two major conceptions of the depression current during the 1930's. Relying upon one of the fundamental conclusions of the classical economic tradition, many observers continued to regard the economy as a self-regulating mechanism which normally tended toward efficient and full use of human and other productive resources. In their opinion the depression therefore was the result of malfunction; explaining the depression was akin to locating the flawed part in a poorly operating engine.

In the early stages of the Great Depression, during the long nightmare descent of 1929–1933 with its waves of bank failures and its rapidly mounting unemployment, popular explanations located the source of malfunction in some impressive and tangible event or aberration of human behavior. Three interpretations of this sort, each emphasizing a different factor as the cause of the economy's derangement, appear at the beginning of the first group of readings. The first two selections, one by Ambrose Benkert, the second by Harold G. Moulton, trace the dislocations in the American economic structure to events in Europe. A third selection, by the psychologist John J. B.

Morgan, interprets the depression as the consequence of mass psychosis. His view, though it seems farfetched today, enjoyed considerable popularity during the early '30's.

In the face of the shockingly severe downswing of 1929–1933 and the appalling stagnation of the economy during the remainder of the depression decade, such explanations began to seem superficial. Soon economists began a search to locate more deep-rooted causes for the malfunction of the economy. The readings in the second section of Part I are representative of the theorizing which resulted. Arthur B. Adams, a well-known economist writing in 1932, gave a convincing form to the notion, already embraced by many popular commentators but considered disreputable by most economists, that a general imbalance between production and consumption had developed within the economy. Partisans of the "overproduction-underconsumption" thesis looked to structural reforms, such as growth in consumer purchasing power through an increase in wage rates, to achieve balance between output and consumption and thus to restore satisfactory performance of the self-regulating economy of the predepression era. And like President Roosevelt in his "Fireside Chat" of 1938, they also advocated government spending to bolster purchasing power. In the two readings following the Adams and Roosevelt articles, Gardiner Means and H. L. McCracken also posit structural impairment as the root of economic breakdown. Instead of an imbalance between production and consumption, however, they identify internal rigidities caused by the monopoly power of business as the fatal flaw in the economic framework.

Part II contains selections representing the other major conception of the depression familiar in the '30's. This school of thought regarded the historic economy not merely as a mechanism which, when operating properly, produced goods and services at one particular level, but as a dynamic system whose prosperity had always depended upon continuous expansion. The severity and long duration of the depression betokened, in this view, the end of American economic growth. The "maturity thesis" of the earlier '30's, represented by an *Iron Age* editorial and by excerpts from President Roosevelt's speeches of 1932–33, defined the depression as the transition between an expanding and a mature economy, centering on the simple notion that the economy's capacity to produce had, in an absolute sense, outrun its capacity to consume. The *Iron Age* article, however, suggests cooperation of businessmen in a noncompetitive system as a remedy for the problems of transition, whereas Roosevelt stressed the need for drastic changes in government policy.

The "secular stagnation" thesis of the later '30's used the same basic appraisal of the depression in a more sophisticated manner. By this time many American economists had learned from the writings of their European counterparts, especially from John Maynard Keynes' *General Theory of Employment*, to regard the level of investment (that is, business spending on new plant and equipment) as the key determinant of the economy's performance. They had learned also, still following Keynesian logic, to accept an idea which formerly prevailing economic theory had deemed impossible, the fact that an economic system need not tend toward full employment but can establish an equilibrium far short of the optimum level of activity.

Adopting these theories, Alvin Hansen, the most noted protagonist of the "secular stagnation" thesis, was able to present with chilling plausibility a picture of the depression as the end of American economic growth. America's traditional prosperity, Hansen argued, had reflected a rapid rate of growth nourished by the seemingly limitless investment opportunities provided by an unsettled continent and a high rate of population increase. These stimulants had disappeared, Hansen believed. Appropriate governmental policies could relieve the resulting stagnation in some degree, but, and this was the most appalling of Hansen's conclusions, perhaps only at the expense of traditional economic and political liberties. The stagnationist theory, stating that adequate living standards can be maintained only through income redistribution, public spending for welfare purposes, and similar policies undertaken on a grand scale, was hotly debated during the late '30's and the World War II period. The selection authored by Glenn McLaughlin and Ralph Watkins serves as an example of the concrete arguments used by Hansen's followers to buttress his theory.

Perhaps the most significant contemporary rejoinder to the stagnationists came from Joseph A. Schumpeter. His argument, published originally in 1939, is the last selection in Part II. Schumpeter's writings before and after the coming of the Great Depression were largely responsible for introducing to American economists the view that depression was only a downturn in the capitalist process of economic growth. To the partisan of the stagnation thesis the long duration of the depression signified that the American economy's capacity for growth was exhausted; Schumpeter rejected this conclusion. Instead, he attributed the low level of economic activity in the '30's to the timidity of investors and

managers generated by social atmosphere and the New Deal's reforms, denying any lack of underlying investment opportunities and growth capacity in the economy. Nevertheless, Schumpeter's prognosis of the future of American capitalism was nearly as pessimistic as that of the secular stagnationists. The periodic instability inherent in the capitalist growth process, Schumpeter concluded, leads to political demands for institutional reform which hinder recovery and ultimately smother the ability of the traditional capitalist economy to perform successfully.

Without accepting his ultimate gloomy conclusions about the effects of the New Deal's reforms upon American capitalism, modern interpreters of the Great Depression, represented in Part III, have for the most part taken as the basis for their analyses Schumpeter's thesis that the depression was only a hiatus in the growth process. The economy's steady progress during the postwar decades has encouraged the present generation of economists to reexamine the wellsprings of investment opportunities and to conclude, as Ernst W. Swanson does, that they are far from dried up. The selection by John Kenneth Galbraith serves to emphasize the fact that, although contemporary economists regard the Great Depression as a serious lapse in the historic progression of the American economy, they continue to acknowledge the contribution of institutional weaknesses to the economic debacle. The concluding articles explore the question of why the normal growth processes of American capitalism failed to take hold during the '30's. John Chamberlain makes an interesting analysis of underlying technological investment in the American economy during the 1930's that was qualitatively impressive, even though total investment remained quantitatively lower than needed to restore full employment until mobilization began. Robert Gordon argues in detail that a failure of investment opportunities did indeed occur in the depression decade, but that the failure was only temporary, being attributable to the exploitation of investment in the '20's, the timidity of investors after the financial liquidation of 1929, and the relative inflexibility of some prices.

All four articles in this final group of readings raise meaningful questions that we must take into account in any discussion of the historic pattern of American economic development and the structure of modern American capitalism.

CONTENTS

The Clash of Issues

Many contemporaries of the depression interpreted it as a result of imbalance or malfunction in the economic machine:

From 1923 to 1929 our economic system was thrown out of balance. During this period we increased our power to produce goods, especially per worker, while at the same time the distribution of the current money income or power to purchase these goods became more unequal and maladjusted. This lack of balance was overcome temporarily through the unsound use of bank credit in creating buying power and therefore the demand for goods. The artificial prosperity thus generated could not last forever. The maladjustment between the production of goods and the distribution of income finally showed itself in the present depression.

ARTHUR B. ADAMS

Other contemporaries saw the depression as the end of economic expansion, or "secular stagnation":

The swift stream of events in the last quarter century offers, however, overwhelming testimony in support of the thesis that the economic order of the western world is undergoing in this generation a structural change no less basic and profound in character than that transformation of economic life and institutions which we are wont to designate loosely by the phrase "the Industrial Revolution." We are passing, so to speak, over a divide which separates the great era of growth and expansion of the nineteenth century from an era which no man, unwilling to embark on pure conjecture, can as yet characterize with clarity or precision. We are moving swiftly out of the order in which those of our generation were brought up, into no one knows what.

ALVIN HANSEN

Modern economists provide a more eclectic and balanced view:

[S]tagnation existed in the 1930's, but . . . it did not necessarily have secular significance. Investment opportunities were restricted then because they had been so thoroughly exploited in the 1920's and because the severity of the financial liquidation after 1929 led businessmen and investors to view with a jaundiced eye the opportunities that were available. We would add that, given such a situation, the relative inflexibility of some prices (for example, building costs) prevented investment from being as high as it might otherwise have been. And, as noted before, the reaction of business to New Deal policies made the situation still worse.

ROBERT GORDON

I. THE DEPRESSION AS MALFUNCTION OF THE SELF-REGULATING ECONOMY

Ambrose W. Benkert: THE DEPRESSION AS AN AFTERMATH
OF WORLD WAR I

*Benkert, an investment counselor and a prominent member of the
New York State Chamber of Commerce, wrote a brief text for a popular
pamphlet series in 1933 which related the depression to the First World
War. Though unpolished in style and economic reasoning, Benkert's
pamphlet, from which the following selection is excerpted, is an excellent illustration of an argument which was widely accepted during the
early years of the depression.*

IT [IS] evident that the existing paralysis of business in the United States
is due primarily to a breakdown of fair
price interrelationships among commodities, raw materials, manufactured goods
and services.

By *fair price relationship* is meant such
relationship as prevailed when general
prosperity existed. Prosperity is the automatic result of a maximum exchange of
goods and services — and such maximum
interchange is never attained excepting
when it is made possible by a fair price
relationship between the values to be
exchanged.

DISTORTED PRICE LEVELS

The present disparity in price relationships is quite generally evident. Example:
The present price level of commodities
and raw materials in contrast with the
price level of essential services as expressed in taxes, interest and maturing
debts, rents, transportation and utility
rates. Many commodity and raw material
prices, subject to the inexorable law of
supply and demand, are at the lowest

levels in a century. Essential services depending on contract or governmental fixation still enjoy the peak price level of
recent years.

As a result of such distorted price
levels, the producer of commodities and
raw materials, after meeting his taxes,
debt services, and obtaining the bare
essentials of existence, has nothing left
to exchange for manufactured goods and
other services. In consequence, factories
become idle, commerce deteriorates, unemployment increases, and the depression grows by what it feeds on.

At this point the question arises: What
has caused the present disparity in
prices?

The answer calls for a summary of economic events since the last period when
normal relationships existed. This period
is found in the years immediately before
the World War. During those years price
relationships were fairly well in balance
and there was relatively little unemployment throughout the civilized world.

The World War distorted the entire
picture and led quickly to a series of

From Ambrose W. Benkert, *How to Restore Values. The Quick, Safe Way Out of the Depression*
(*The John Day Pamphlets, No. 23*) (New York: The John Day Co., 1933), pp. 6–11. Reprinted by
permission of Mrs. Ambrose W. Benkert.

maladjustments. The first effect on price levels was felt in commodities and raw materials, followed promptly by increasing prices for manufactured goods, especially for those required to prosecute the war. Labor soon found its compensation inadequate, and as a result of strikes or voluntary adjustments wages were increased to cope with the new price level. And last of all, service charges subject to contract and governmental fixation were advanced to bring the whole price level once again fairly well into balance. In consequence, we emerged from the war on an entirely different plateau of price levels.

POSTWAR READJUSTMENTS

Return of the warring populations to civil pursuits again occasioned a distortion of the price picture. A spasmodic, violent drop occurred in the price level of primary goods and a variety of manufactures, and the first postwar readjustments followed.

The falling trend of prices was promptly arrested and reversed, however, by huge loans to foreign nations, beginning as early as 1919. These loans were made possible by the fact that during the war the United States had changed from a debtor to a preponderantly creditor nation. During the postwar decade loans amounting to many billions of dollars were made, and most of the civilized nations of the world became our debtors.

It is interesting to note at this point that the amount of such loans, plus our tourist expenditures, closely paralleled our exports. This accounts for the anomaly of a creditor nation continuing to maintain an export balance.

Confidence engendered by the election of Mr. Coolidge in 1924 and adoption of the Dawes Plan for Germany in the same year added the nations evolved from the Central Empires to the recipients of our loans. Huge amounts were advanced to these countries during the next four years, thus helping to maintain and advance our foreign and domestic price level.

During the same period, 1924–28, many of the foreign nations were enabled to resume the gold standard primarily because of the loans from the United States.

SPECULATION SHUTS OFF LOANS

The increased prosperity, resulting largely from adding the Central Empires countries to our customers during this period, was promptly reflected in increased earnings of our domestic corporations. The common stocks of these companies began to advance in price, and with this advance the appetite of investors for equity stocks became so whetted that the whole nation was caught up in a frenzy of speculation in the latter part of 1928.

For a year and a half before the crash of 1929 our investors generally lost interest in fixed obligations. Their capital was employed almost exclusively in speculation not only in stocks but in all other forms of value. The issuing of foreign bonds in the American market practically ceased.

Foreign nations were therefore compelled to curtail imports and expand exports to provide funds for service charges on these external loans. Most of the nations which had borrowed from us were primarily producers of commodities and raw materials and were our best customers for manufactured goods. In many of these countries programs were initiated to reduce the quantity of commodities used by their own populations in order to have a greater supply for export, and at the same time their own manufactures were stimulated so as to reduce imports and provide additional exports to equalize their balance of payments.

PRICES FALL, TARIFFS RISE, WORLD BIDS FOR GOLD

These policies, initiated even before the crash of 1929, started a world-wide downward trend of commodity prices, slowed up the demand for our own manufactures, and intensified competition with us in our domestic and foreign markets.

An attempt was then made to meet this situation by increasing our tariffs. This only intensified the struggle through retaliatory higher tariffs, trade restrictions, quotas and allotments on the part of our foreign debtor nations.

These policies so restricted and curtailed international trade that our debtor nations were compelled to meet their debt services mainly by shipping gold. The consequent drain of gold impaired the gold coverage of the currencies of one country after another, forcing them to suspend specie payment — in other words, to "abandon the gold standard" — until only the United States and France, Switzerland, Holland and Belgium remained.

In short, our policies compelled our foreign debtor nations to *bid for gold,* and thus increase the value of gold in terms of their own exports; or, conversely, decrease the value of their exports in terms of gold. This procedure cumulatively broke down world price levels and flooded all markets with cheaper and cheaper goods.

Being on a gold basis, and our currency therefore being equivalent to gold, our price levels for commodities, raw materials and other goods in world competition generally speaking declined proportionately. Our domestic price levels for services and goods depending on contract, governmental fixation, usage, trade combinations, etc., remained where they were. *Thus was brought about the disparity in price levels within our own country.*

Inasmuch as over 90 per cent of our business activity consists of interchange of goods and services within the United States, it is apparent that our present business stagnation is due primarily to this maladjustment of domestic price levels.

Conversely, a restoration of our own business and prosperity depends primarily upon the restoration of a fair domestic price relationship. Such prosperity will, of course, be materially augmented by a restoration of world trade. The latter obviously depends upon removal of trade restrictions and facilitation of maximum international exchange of goods and services.

The immediate problem therefore is to find the way to restore relatively fair domestic price relationships. How can this be accomplished?

Harold G. Moulton: AMERICAN DEPENDENCE ON
EUROPEAN MARKETS

*Harold G. Moulton's career as a professional economist began in
1914 when he assumed a teaching post at the University of Chicago.
In this capacity and after 1928 as President of the Brookings Institution,
a well-known economic research organization, Moulton gained recognition as a leading commentator on current economic problems. In the
following article, given originally as a radio address on the NBC radio
network on October 31, 1931, Moulton presented a cogent statement of
the view held in one form or another by many observers — that American recovery depended upon restoration of her export markets.*

THE RECENT series of financial
crises in European countries and
the ensuing repercussions upon American finance and American foreign trade
have brought a new realization of the
economic unity of the world and of the
degree to which American prosperity is
linked with that of Europe. It is a curi-
ous fact, when one pauses to think about
it, that this economic interdependency
is apparent to the average observer only
in periods of business reaction. During
the recent boom era, for example, the
view was very widespread that the
United States had proved her economic
independence of the rest of the world —
that within our broad economic domain
we had achieved economic self-suffi-
ciency as well as discovered the secret of
permanent prosperity. The relation between the expanding business of other
countries during those years — an expansion made possible in large measure by
American foreign loans — and American
prosperity was so obscure as to be almost
entirely ignored. But once the world-
depression got under way and our export
trade began to shrink, with accompanying disastrous effects upon the prices of
our primary export products, it quickly
became clear that our vaunted economic
independence was without foundation.

The extent to which our exports to
Europe have shrunk is, however, even
now not fully appreciated. In the years
1926 to 1929 the value of our European
shipments ranged around $2,300,000,000,
annually. In 1930 it declined to $1,-
800,000,000; and during the first half of
1931 the value fell to a yearly rate of
$1,200,000,000. Each succeeding month
since March has shown further shrink-
age, and the shipments to Europe are
now smaller than in 1913 — in actual volume as well as in terms of value.

It is reasonably clear from these figures
that a fundamental requirement, if we
are to have a return of real prosperity,
is the stabilization of European financial
conditions and the promotion of economic recovery there. I do not mean to
imply that a business revival could not
under any circumstances have its begin-
nings in the United States and then
spread by gradual stages to the rest of
the world. But I do mean that chaotic
financial, economic, and social conditions
such as exist in Europe at this juncture
present a virtually insuperable barrier to
economic recovery in this country. Con-

Harold G. Moulton, *America and the Balance Sheet of Europe: An Address . . . in the Economics
Series Sponsored by the National Council on Radio in Education* (University of Chicago Press,
1931), pp. 1–9.

structive efforts toward world economic recuperation must therefore be focused upon Europe.

Before attempting to suggest ways in which an improvement in European economic conditions may be promoted, we must seek to appraise the nature of the economic difficulties with which central and western Europe have been confronted, not only in recent months but throughout the post-war era. It is fully appreciated by people everywhere that the World War resulted in an enormous destruction of wealth. But of greater importance — and this is not commonly recognized — were the economic and trade maladjustments which occurred. The normal economic balance between Europe and other countries, particularly the United States, was destroyed.

During the course of the World War the agriculture, the industry, and the finances of the European belligerents were thoroughly disorganized. In other countries, however, production and trade were expanded beyond all known bounds. The European shortage of commodities, coupled with an intensified demand, served like a protective tariff to stimulate new industries in nearly every non-belligerent country. This was true not only of the neutral nations of Europe, but the influence extended to North and South America, Australia, and the Orient as well. Moreover, agricultural production was enormously extended, particularly in Canada and the United States.

After the war was over the European belligerents naturally and of necessity sought to rehabilitate both their agriculture and their industry. The resuscitation of European agriculture which commenced shortly after the war inevitably lessened the demand for American and Canadian foodstuffs and precipitated an agricultural depression which has continued throughout the post-war era, even during periods of industrial prosperity.

The gradual industrial rehabilitation of Europe on the one hand lessens the demand for imported manufactured commodities, and on the other hand increases the European exports of manufactured goods. General economic recovery of Europe necessitates the recapture by the exporters of that continent of many formerly established markets, for the manufacturing nations of Europe depend upon exports of finished goods as a means of paying for imports of raw materials and foodstuffs.

It is readily apparent that such a process of recovery has not been welcome to those nations whose productive capacity has been so greatly expanded during the World War period. While the European nations have sought industrial and trade readjustments, other countries have endeavored to prevent such readjustment and to maintain the position which they had gained during the war. It is this fundamental conflict which accounts for the erection of new tariff barriers since the war and for the inability of the leading nations, either through their governments or international business organizations, to find a basis for harmonious international trade policies.

These fundamental trade difficulties accompanying the rising and falling of the economic tides produced by the World War have, moreover, been intensified as a result of the *financial* consequences of the war. In the first place, in the war and early post-war years the balance of international trade and financial relations was so profoundly altered that the private investors in these European nations lost a substantial part of their previously accumulated foreign holdings. With most nations the position shifted from that of creditor to that of debtor and in some instances, notably in the case of Germany, practically all foreign investments were lost. On the other hand, in the United States and Japan, Holland and the Scandinavian countries, and to a lesser extent elsewhere, the reverse occurred and these countries emerged as substantial creditors.

In addition to these great shifts in the balance of private international indebtedness, the war left a legacy of huge international governmental indebtedness. While the inter-allied indebtedness was incurred for value received, these wartime loans were not productive in character. Moreover, the reparation obligations imposed by the treaties of peace upon the Central Powers bore no relation whatever to economic enterprise. They were simply fines imposed for damages sustained.

The significance of these shifts in the relative financial position of the European belligerents is to be found in the long-run trade readjustments which the new relationships necessarily involve. A debtor nation must, if it is to meet its interest obligations, in the long run export more than it imports — this in order to obtain the foreign exchange with which to pay interest instalments abroad. Now the debtor countries, because of the maladjustments of the war period, to which reference has already been made, find it extremely difficult to earn the foreign exchange with which to meet their debts. The efforts of other countries to protect the new industries which developed during the war and to maintain their own exports inevitably handicap the exporting possibilities of the debtor countries.

The situation is particularly complex as it relates to the United States. This country's economic machine is geared to produce an enormous flow of goods for export — both agricultural commodities and industrial products. If our productive capacity is to be fully and efficiently employed, we need to maintain large exports. On the other hand, we have been endeavoring to keep imports at a minimum, our tariff being designed to protect American industry, and to a lesser extent agriculture, from foreign competition. Thus, we strive to maintain a large export surplus when the economic requirements of reparation and war-debt payments necessitate an import surplus.

During recent years we have temporarily avoided the dilemma of collecting debts, without receiving an excess of imports, by means of new loans to Europe. That is to say, instead of getting out of debt, Europe — speaking generally — has been going even further into debt. To illustrate by reference to Germany — the nation which is supposed to provide the wealth for the liquidation of all the war debts — that country has since the inauguration of the Dawes Plan in 1924 borrowed about two dollars for every dollar paid on reparation account. It has been the thought — or rather the hope — that this process might be continued indefinitely, thereby avoiding at least until some remote future day the trade readjustments that are required if the reparation obligation is finally to be collected.

These huge loans, amounting between 1924 and 1930 to approximately $4,000,-000,000, moreover obscured the basic economic problems of Germany. For the time being the loans promoted buoyant economic activity and prevented any possible exchange crisis. It was thus possible for superficial observers to believe that Germany had completely recovered from the war, and also that it had been demonstrated that both the reparation and inter-allied debt obligations could be met according to schedule without in anywise adversely affecting our trade.

But it was only a few months after new credits ceased to be extended that Germany's finances broke down and the country was threatened with a repetition of the tragic conditions of 1923. Emphasis is placed upon the German situation because it is at the heart of the whole problem of the war debts, the inter-allied debt payments having been closely articulated with reparation receipts.

With the prompt and courageous policy announced by this government last June in favor of a complete moratorium on reparation and inter-allied debt payments for the period of a year, this vexatious problem entered upon a new phase. As a result of the economic events of the past year, we are now in a position to consider more clearly than ever before the economics of this problem. The fundamental question is whether our own prosperity and that of the world as a whole will best be promoted by eliminating so far as possible those factors which produce unbalanced trade relations and by enlarging European purchasing power. It needs to be clearly borne in mind in this connection that every dollar which the European nations turn over to us in liquidation of war-time obligations means a dollar that cannot be used by them to purchase American exports. Reduced purchases of our products

means reduced prices of export commodities, and these in turn mean decreased earnings and decreased tax-paying capacity on the part of American agriculture and American industry. While our export trade accounts for a relatively small percentage of our total trade, its curtailment leads to severe depression of basically important industries, and this in turn has its repercussions upon the entire business structure. The potential tax revenues that might be collected from profitable American business greatly outweigh the gains to the Treasury from the collection of war debts.

Thoroughgoing economic recovery in the United States is not to be expected until financial stability can be established in Europe and until the financial and trade maladjustments which resulted from the World War are in substantial measure eliminated. Some of the maladjustments produced by the war cannot be readily overcome. But the artificial ones resulting from the war debts may be eliminated — difficult though the political aspects of the problem still are. In conclusion, I would emphasize again the basic fact that a state of balanced trade between Europe and America is a prime essential for the prosperity of both continents.

John J. B. Morgan: MANIC-DEPRESSIVE PSYCHOSES OF BUSINESS

John J. B. Morgan, for many years Professor of Psychology at North-western University and a recognized authority in the field of abnormal psychology, presented the following appraisal of the depression in his presidential address before the Midwestern Psychological Association in May 1934.

EMERGING as we are from a very extreme business depression, with the worst probably over, we should be able to make a relatively cool analysis of the symptoms which were manifest while business was in the midst of a major phase of a manic-depressive psychosis.

This paper proceeds from the premise that business is subject to various psychoses which need analysis by psychologically trained persons and, in support of this premise, proposes the consideration of business depressions as illustrative of a psychological interpretation of one syndrome.

Looked at from close range there is a temptation to believe that what we have witnessed is an isolated event due to some sort of calamity which produced a disruption of normal business. Taking a sufficient period of time to give us an adequate perspective, it is apparent that business has gradually been developing a functional instability which is growing into more and more clean-cut demonstrations of psychotic symptoms which are strangely similar to the symptoms of manic-depressive psychosis in the individual.

Whatever our diagnosis may be, we must admit that business has been sick and we must also admit that there is profound ignorance as to the cause, the significance of the symptoms manifested, the treatments that should be applied, and the prognosis for the disease. As in all cases where ignorance abounds we have no dearth of theories to explain the various symptoms. We have all sorts of remedies suggested, most of them quack remedies; indeed one person has called this the quack remedy stage of modern business.

It is well known, in the case of a manic-depressive psychosis in an individual, that the patient usually recovers in spite of any and all treatments to which he is subjected. After such recovery every person who had anything to do with the patient can lay claim to credit for the cure and, doubtless, after a complete recovery from the recent depressed phase of the business cycle, we shall hear all sorts of claims as to the efficiency of certain measures which were used. The history of modern business leads one to believe that there would have been a recovery no matter what had been done. The recovery of the patient is never a valid argument in favor of the treatment given.

Consequently, our aim is not to suggest some new quack remedy, but to make an analysis of some of the symptoms. We shall attempt to show that business is suffering from a functional psychosis which has its roots in the emotional conflicts of the business organism. Our method will be the case study method.

From John J. B. Morgan, "Manic-Depressive Psychoses of Business," *Psychological Review*, Vol. XLII, 1 (January 1935), pp. 91–93, 98–107.

It is fairly well agreed that the depression through which business is just passing is not an isolated symptom but a phase of a more or less rhythmical up and down movement which has been given the name business cycle. Furthermore, the characteristic business cycle as we know it today, with its wild speculation and abnormal depressions, has been apparent only since the development of an elaborate money economy.

From the middle of the eighteenth century to the present day, business has shown a cyclical character in which industry rises to a high stage of activity, or boom excitement, until a crash ensues; then there is a period of unemployment, business depression, often culminating in a panic; a recovery, business activity, and finally another boom. With the entrance of the seventeenth century, clear-cut crises as an aftermath of inflation may be found.

Since 1873 we have been becoming more and more business cycle conscious, so much so that newspapers glibly inform readers just what phase of the business cycle we are in at any moment. Governmental agencies have been used to study the causes of business cycle so that steps can be taken to control them. Indeed, before the last business collapse we were told that the whole phenomenon had been analyzed and that the Federal Reserve Board had developed means for controlling cycles. We were in a "new era" and would see no more industrial crises. Such prophetic utterances were nullified by the outbreak of the worst business depression of the century.

❊ ❊ ❊

Practically every symptom of the business cycle has been invoked to explain it. There are theories which put the blame on our capitalistic economy, some which blame our methods of exchange, some which blame our money economy, some which blame it on human psychology. All have facts in their favor but how is one to judge the relative value of them?

While these theories are so diverse that they leave the reader mystified, they have made two very important contributions. They have enabled us to differentiate sharply between organic and functional business psychoses. The older depressions came from external calamities such as earthquakes, plagues, crop failures, plunderings by hostile nations, and the like. Such depressions are not hard to understand. It is not hard to see why the South suffered a depression following the Civil War after she had spent all her money and had her slaves freed. It is easy to comprehend the misfortune of a planter who has his wheat crop destroyed by locusts.

A more important contribution from a study of these theories is the discovery that functional depressions are invariably preceded by business booms. It is clear that the boom and depression must be studied in conjunction as aspects of some central and related process which causes the whole cycle.

The next question that confronts us is the nature of the relationship between the boom and depression. Is it a causal relationship? Does the boom cause the depression or does the depression cause the boom? If both were true, we would have a species of perpetual motion. It is more probable that there is some hidden factor responsible for the entire cycle, or that the hidden factor causes the inflation and the inflation precipitates the collapse and depression.

With the exception of these two findings, the business cycle theorists have been mainly concerned with elaborate descriptions of the various symptoms of the business cycle. They have demonstrated by elaborate statistical studies that during a boom, prices rise, production increases, employment grows, debts increase, interest rates rise, optimism grows, and buildings multiply. All of these fall off in a depression.

There is a great temptation to fall into the error of thinking that an accurate description of these symptoms constitutes an explanation; but it is just as much of an error as to think we have explained a manic-depressive psychosis when we have made careful curves of changes in motor activity, rate of thinking, of emotional reactions, and of bodily temperature in the different cycles through which our patient passes.

A still greater error comes when one attempts to cure the disease by treating symptoms. This latter error we have witnessed in various forms and degrees during the last cycle. As we have said, various warnings were issued before the crash of 1929. The Federal Reserve Board tried to put on the brakes by raising the discount rate, by issuing warnings, and by selling securities. Such restraints were about as futile as applying strait-jackets and restraining devices to our manic patient. They may hold him down somewhat but they do not cure him and may even excite him to further manic behavior. Eventually the crash came and the Reserve Banks reversed their tactics. They lowered the discount rates and bought securities, both of which processes were artificial stimulants to business; but business declined only the faster. Their tactics were just as futile as the administration of artificial stimulants is to the depressed patient in the psychopathic hospital. Then attempts were made to cheer up the jaded nerves of business men by optimistic pronouncements by various leaders of political parties and business enterprises but with about as much effect as optimistic statements have upon a depressed person. Prosperity being around the corner became a joke. With each such pronouncement our business patient slumped the more. Then the group that had been imbued with the over-saving philosophy of Foster and Catchings had their inning and people were urged to spend and buy their way back to prosperity. This makes one think of the optimist who tells the depressed patient to get up and dance so that his gloom may vanish. Then we were told that we had produced too much so we turned under our crops and killed pigs on the theory that we must have rising prices to bring back prosperity. Such destruction, however, did not enable the jobless to buy what was left after the destruction. So we were told that the trouble was with the distribution of wealth and that, by taxation, we must extract the savings from the thrifty and give jobs to those who had nothing. But these who were given jobs must not produce or we would have another glut on the market so they must be given such useless jobs as scraping dirt on and off our highways. Finally, the symptom of too little money had to be remedied by cutting down the content of the dollar. This latter treatment reminds the writer of the trick played by a father on his son who was in deep emotional depression because he wanted two pieces of candy instead of the one he possessed. The father broke the candy into two pieces and told the boy that he now had his wish — to dry his tears.

In the meanwhile, our business patient has been showing signs of recovery. Is the recovery taking place because of any one of these applications of theory, because of a combination of them, or in spite of them? We hear arguments for all three of these possibilities.

It may be necessary in an emergency to deal with symptoms. Business has been sick and anything that can be done to alleviate the pain may be justified. The danger comes when dealing with superficial symptoms becomes our goal.

Is it possible to get behind these diverse symptoms which manifest themselves in a manic-depressive psychosis of business and to discover the underlying factors which cause the disease? Perhaps we can get our answer, if we discover why men go to the speculative excesses which characterize a boom period.

The reason that is commonly given for the excessive optimism which leads to a business boom is lack of sound judgment. Men become blinded by false hopes and cease to be guided by their better judgment. Certainly the last boom was not accompanied by ignorance. Business men were aware that things were moving at too fast a pace. The newspapers and financial magazines warned that brokers' loans to the extent of eight or nine billions of dollars were excessive. The great amount of future income that was tied up with installment buying was known to contain a dire threat to the financial soundness of the country. The Federal Reserve Board issued warnings, raised the discount rate, and sold securities in an attempt to curb the wild speculation, but in vain. Certainly the cause was not ignorance.

BUSINESS MANIA CAUSED BY FEAR

We believe that it is fear that drives men to wild speculation, just as it is fear that drives men into manic flights in manic-depressive psychoses. Manic-depressive patients become emotionally elated because they are running away from some internal conflict which they dare not face and from which they have learned to defend themselves through distraction by trivial incidents of life, by excessive activity, by the excitement of running into uncertainty, and by forced happiness. While a close analogy may be dangerous, we think that a business mania may be interpreted in a similar fashion.

In the final stages of a boom, the wild speculator does not imagine that prices will go up forever, that business will continue to rise indefinitely. He may preach a "new-day" but his preaching is a whistling in the dark to allay his own fears. He knows that there will be an end to the boom, that the turning point will come but with each fear he plunges deeper, trusting to fate that he will get out just before the turning point comes. A boom is not a period of over-optimism; the optimism is an artificial device, an attempt to hide the underlying fear.

It is this fear factor which makes the crash so violent when it does arrive. Everybody gets "jittery"; the swings on the stock market become extreme, and those who think they are prudent place stop-loss orders. When the break finally comes these stop-loss orders pile up so fast that they cannot be executed. Everybody is wildly trying to sell and everybody is afraid to buy. Sometimes it takes but the slightest shock to start the downward plunge, a situation which could not develop if everybody were optimistic, if the excessive activity did not hide an underlying fear.

Not all fears cause psychoses. A direct fear of some concrete danger is handled by dealing with the cause of the fear. As long as we are fighting a fear-producing situation, we are mentally sound; and if business could always be fighting in the open there would never be any business psychoses. There would be changes in the tide of fortune but there would not be insane manias and equally insane depressions.

What is this subconscious fear which lurks behind all business and produces psychotic symptoms? We believe that this fear is to be found in the shaky nature of our credit system. Such fears were *not* a part of the old barter system. Under such an economy each man had tangible evidence of his possessions. He either had stores of goods or he had their equivalent in money which, in itself, had intrinsic value and which he could be sure, at any time, was transferable into other goods. Business was done on a cash basis; and the cash that was used had intrinsic value. His only fears were of very evident dangers; such as having his goods or his money stolen or being worsted in a trade.

Today at least ninety per cent of our business is done on credit and what money we do have has no intrinsic value. It is simply the promise of the government to pay — not in gold or anything of value but in other dollars of the same sort. The entire business structure is built upon promises to pay.

Let us see how a small gold reserve held by a government can be used as a foundation for a very shaky credit pyramid. A government with, say, two billion dollars in gold, issues paper money to the extent of four to six billion dollars, and bonds — which we are told are payable in gold — to the extent of ten billions more. These money tokens and bonds are placed with banks and represent security for commercial loans made to customers. The loans are not in actual money but in bank credits upon which the borrower issues checks. Personal checks issued on the basis of such loans are passed from buyer to seller and are, in effect, money. With only two billions

of gold in some central storehouse, a country can do business which runs into hundreds of billions of dollars a year.

What a difference in the faith needed to operate such a credit system as we have and that manifested by the old traders each of whom held on to his possession until he had a firm grip on the object he was to receive and both dropped their hold upon one of the objects after counting: one — two — three!

The credit system is a system built upon faith, but faith in what or in whom? As this point we come to the element in modern business which we believe to be the cause of the manic-depressive psychosis of business. It is a lack of insight, or a lack of candor, as in what or in whom we are actually putting our trust when we extend or accept credit. We have a belief that we are continuing to put our trust in gold in the same manner that we did when we traded for cash and received gold in payment. Our contracts are all written as though they would ultimately be paid in gold coin, but they are written in such excessive amounts that they can *never* be paid in gold coin. The fact that, in recent years, whenever there was a money stringency, every country involved had to suspend gold payments is enough evidence of that fact. We think we have money on deposit in banks, but, were all depositors to claim their money today, there would not be enough money in the world to pay them. It is illegal to possess a gold dollar at this time and yet we conduct business as though it were on a gold basis. This is the self-deceit which is the basis of the disintegration of business.

Yet without faith in something business could not go on at all. What is it that men trust when they do business? Their trust is in two things: First, that business will continue to go on. They have faith in the world as a going concern. Secondly, they have faith that men will, on the whole, fulfill the contracts they have made either through force of laws or through their own integrity.

If the only essential was to believe that business would continue, business cycles would be of minor extent. Business men would try to foresee all contingencies, and would ajust accordingly. They would make preparations for changes just as we make preparations for changes in weather based on all the information we can gather. With this one element operative, we would have business cycles but they would not be the extreme cycles which we have been describing.

On the other hand, our faith in men and in our modern institutions is not solid enough to resist fluctuations. Business oscillations are due to the ebb and flow of our faith in them. When we become skeptical of the integrity of our fellows or our government we want to run to the cover of a gold standard; we want to contract our credit. When we see the government borrowing more than she can ever pay back, we begin to entertain grave doubts. Such a situation obtains, for example, after an expensive war. When municipalities, corporations, and private individuals all appear to be taking upon themselves more and more obligations, the fear and distrust of any far-seeing man will begin to accumulate.

But what can he do? He may have growing fears but he cannot stop. His very business existence depends upon continuing in activity, so he drives himself to more activity to meet the growing mistrust within him. The manufacturer makes greater and greater quantities of goods at thinner and thinner profits, hoping that he can get rid of his products faster than the other fellow and that he can pile up enough reserves to tide him through the lean years that he knows will come. He piles up a greater and greater cash surplus because he knows he must gird himself for the impending slump. This money is placed in reserve centers to be loaned to others who must expand their business because of the same fear motive. Goods must be somehow sold, so all sorts of time payments are arranged, and these depend on the hopes of the buyers that they can hold their jobs. But their very jobs depend upon the ability of producers to sell an increasing quantity of goods to an increasingly satiated public.

BOOMS ARE DEFENSIVE MECHANISMS

The boom is a mania, a defense mechanism, functioning to hide the ever-rising tide of fears. Fears drive to further activity and further activity increases the fear, moving in an upward spiral which becomes more and more unstable.

A boom is a psychological affair; it is a problem in human emotions which have grown to pathological proportions. Once a boom gets started it soon gets out of hand and must run its course in the same manner that a manic-depressive psychosis must run its course in the individual. That course is an inevitable mania with a reaction to deep depression. Cures cannot be applied during the course of such a cycle; all that can be done is to make the patient as comfortable as possible until the disease has run its course. But after he is over the mania and the succeeding depression, steps can be taken to prevent a recurrence of similar attacks.

Economists are working out methods of measuring public confidence in their attempt to predict what is going to happen so that they may take advantage of the turns; but taking advantage of the turns is quite another problem from removing the causes of insane extremes. It reminds one of the way one group of men took advantage of the manic-depressive cycles of one of their major executives. They studied him so that they knew the signs of a change and could predict his spells of elation and depression. They organized the business so as to place him in strategic positions when he was in a manic mood; and he could accomplish miracles at such times. When they foresaw a depression they would put him at a task where he could do no harm until he recovered. Economists talk as though they would like to keep business in a state of continual mania. To them it seems too bad that there must be a depression and they think the mania causes the depression. We have tried to show that the depression does not cause the mania nor the mania the depression; both result from our unstable credit structure — the breeder of fear, and this fear causes both groups of symptoms in turn.

After the cause of a psychosis is found there are two ways of curing the malady. One is to provide a substitute defense; a sublimation, a better defense mechanism, or some better solution of the conflict. The other is to remove the cause — in this case the fear of insecurity because of distrust in the credit system.

Today the government is attempting to remove the distrust by changing credit from private and corporate hands to the hands of the government. To what extent they have gone in this direction may be seen from the fact that today 98 per cent of the Federal Reserve Credit outstanding is in government financing. Whereas in 1930 about equal amounts of Reserve Credit was invested in bills discounted and government securities, now 50 times as much is placed in government securities as in commercial dis-

counts. In other words, faith in the government is being used to offset lack of faith in industrial and business enterprises. When faith is restored in the ability of business to prosper the tide will turn. A danger in this procedure, it may be pointed out, is the well-known fact that the more any institution borrows the more it reduces its credit and the less faith it deserves. Our government may be able to stand the credit strain but it will have to pay off the debts in some fashion. Besides, most crises have been precipitated, in the first place, by unwise expansion of credit by governments on account of war-borrowings.

In other words, the present emergency measures are no more getting at the cause of the trouble than pouring tonics of iron, quinine, and strychnine into a depressed patient would be. We have blithely built a civilization on promises that our children and grandchildren would pay the bills. Then we try to forget the crime thus perpetrated on our unborn offspring by losing ourselves in manic flights and fits of depression. If we are ever to remove the cause, we need a group of leaders who are heroic enough to pay our bills instead of contracting more. The only final solution is an economy where — if the occasion arose — everybody could pay off his obligations in a very short space of time. There would then be no occasion for the hidden fear which now underlies all business that a day of accounting might come, nor the consequent desire to run to cover so as to beat the other fellow, driven by the knowledge that only the first few to arrive at the goal will remain alive economically.

Since this looks like an impossible utopian idea in the present state of affairs, the only other alternative is to adopt a defense mechanism different from the manic defensive episodes. We have no new defense mechanism or sublimation to suggest. We submit that this is a psychological problem and leave it to this group of psychologists to propose such a substitute.

Arthur B. Adams: MONOPOLY POWER OF BUSINESS AND THE LAG OF PURCHASING POWER

In the campaign of 1932, Herbert Hoover maintained the position which he and most informed commentators on economic affairs had taken during the preceding years of depression: that recovery in America depended upon revival of the international financial and trade system. Franklin Roosevelt, sharply opposing Hoover's interpretation, regarded the depression as essentially the product of domestic influences and therefore as a candidate for remedial action within the national framework. Popular belief had already swung to Roosevelt's viewpoint and soon more and more economists too were exploring defects within the structure of the American economy itself. Among these experts was Arthur B. Adams, Professor of Economics and Dean of the College of Business Administration at the University of Oklahoma. In his Trend of Business, 1922–1932, *published in 1932, Adams produced a polished version of the "overproduction-underconsumption" theory that the economy was generating too little effective purchasing power for the amount of consumers' goods produced. The following selection reproduces the core of his argument.*

CAUSES OF THE BUSINESS DEPRESSION

PRACTICALLY everyone now realizes that the present business depression is not just a state of mind of the public; we have had it firmly impressed upon us that in both cause and effect it is an economic reality. The economic conditions which led up to the depression were somewhat similar to those which have led up to other business depressions; there was increase in production, increase in trade, and considerable inflation in bank credit. From 1923 to 1929 our economic system was thrown out of balance. During this period we increased our power to produce goods, especially per worker, while at the same time the distribution of the current money income or power to purchase these goods became more unequal and maladjusted. This lack of balance was overcome temporarily through the unsound use of bank credit in creating buying power and therefore the demand for goods. The artificial prosperity thus generated could not last forever. The maladjustment between the production of goods and the distribution of income finally showed itself in the present depression. Let us explain how and why this maladjustment came about.

The money proceeds from the net pro-

From pp. 24–29, 30–39, 46–49, 69–70, *Trend of Business 1922–1932* by Arthur B. Adams. Copyright 1932 by Harper & Brothers; renewed 1959 by Arthur B. Adams. Reprinted by permission of Harper & Row, Publishers.

duction of industrial society (the national money income) is distributed in two streams: the first stream is the income going to property owners in the form of royalties, bonuses, interest, rents, and profits which are paid for the use of property, for managerial ability, and for chance gain; the second is the stream of income which is paid to workers in the form of salaries or wages for personal effort in production. A large part of the money income paid to property owners is spent for reinvestment in new capital. Practically all of the money income paid to workers is spent for consumption goods and services. When the part of the national money income going to workers is not large enough to enable them to buy at prevailing prices, the consumers' goods which are unsold tend to pile up in the market. When the part of the national money income going to the property owners is too large, these owners overexpand many industries and over-capitalize practically all of them.

During the years 1922–29 there was a great increase in the physical volume of production of goods of all kinds; and, at the same time, there was a considerable decrease in the "factory" cost of production per unit, due principally to the displacement of labor by machinery and to greater mass production. While there was a slight increase in wage rates, the number of wage earners employed decreased, and the amount of money paid out as wages did not keep pace with the increase in the value of products produced. With a few notable exceptions, the prices of the products produced by industrial enterprises did not decrease in proportion to the decrease in the factory cost of production per unit. This improper adjustment, and the increase in the volume of output, gave much greater profits to business enterprises as a whole, which was the basis for the stock market boom. Lower unit labor cost means that less money is paid to wage earners in proportion to the value of the products produced than was formerly paid to them. Therefore, relative to the annual value of the net product of industry, a larger percentage of the returns was paid to capital and a smaller percentage to labor. As the process continued, the property-owning class was able to command with its current money income a progressively larger percentage of the net product of industry, and the wage-earning class a regressively smaller percentage of the product of industry.

The gain in the relative position of the property-owning class and the loss of the wage-earning class did not for several years adversely affect the equation of the demand for and supply of goods in general. The increase in the demand for goods in general kept pace with the increase in the supply of goods which were placed on the market. During the expansion period, because the larger part of the increase in the income of the property-owning class was used to purchase capital goods rather than consumers' goods, the increase in demand for producers' goods was unquestionably greater than the increase in demand for consumers' goods. Still there was no lagging in the demand for consumers' goods which were offered on the market.

In spite of the relative decrease in the purchasing power of laborers and farmers, the demand for consumers' goods offered on the market (at prevailing prices) until 1929 was sustained by the following forces: (1) Because of the time elements in production, the increase in the flow of consumers' goods to the market was much less rapid than the increase in general production. (2) Consumers' current purchasing power during the period was considerably augmented by the great growth of installment buying. (3) Our large favorable balance of trade, financed largely through the purchase of foreign securities, created a foreign demand for American consumers' goods which were temporarily paid for in part by the saving of the Americans who purchased the foreign securities. (4) The rise in the prices of corporate securities, and the stock market boom, financed partly through increased bank credit, gave a big speculative income to a large group of people who spent part of this inflated income in the purchase of luxury-consumption goods; and (5) during the year 1929 business enterprises withheld part of their finished consumers' goods from the market by accumulating large stocks of goods. By the fall of 1929 all of these artificial supports of the market for consumers' goods were removed, except the accumulation of additional stocks of goods by business enterprises.

If, during the period 1922–29, the prices of fabricated products had been reduced at a slightly greater rate than the rate of decrease in the unit cost of production, the total value of consumers' goods offered in the market would not have increased at a more rapid rate than the flow of consumers' current money income. Under these conditions it would not have been necessary to increase the total wages of laborers. Also, if such a price policy had been followed, agriculture would not have been placed in the disadvantageous position it was. Under those circumstances we would not have had the high profits which were the basis of the stock market boom, the inflation of bank credit and other movements which brought on the depression. But the artificial supports for the market were found, and the prices of fabricated goods were maintained at a relatively stable level.

During the period of expansion of output, a large part of the increased profits from production were invested in new business enterprises and in the enlargement of old ones. Also considerable additional investment funds which went into expansion were drawn from the increases in bank credit. For a considerable time this increased demand for construction goods and producers' goods of all kinds sustained the market for the growing output of factories and shops. It was during this period that some notable economists were explaining to the world that we had reached a higher permanent level of prices, profits and output in this country. Eventually our increased investment in industrial plants began to ripen into an ever-increasing flow of finished consumers' goods and services. It then became necessary to slow down our pace of expansion of construction of all kinds. The markets for both producers' and consumers' goods became heavy, and business enterprise began to cut down their operations. Unemployment increased, this time not because of technological improvements, but because of the reduction in operations. Early in 1929, it became evident that profits of American business corporations would not continue to increase. It later became evident that the profits of these enterprices would not justify the inflated prices of their securities on the Stock Exchange. The Federal Reserve Board began to oppose further use of bank credit to support the inflated prices of securities. The stock market tumbled, and business started on its long slide downward.

*   *   *

The long-standing agricultural depression is related to the present business depression. The small purchasing power of the farming population (due to relatively low prices of agricultural products) since 1920 has adversely affected the demand for consumers' goods in the United States. In spite of this fact, however, the low prices of agricultural products were one of the forces upon which our great industrial expansion (1922–29) fed. The relatively low prices of agricultural products gave manufacturers cheaper raw materials and relieved them of stronger pressure for increases in wages of workers. Low agricultural prices also provided cheap food for the urban population, adding to their relative power to purchase other commodities. Partly as a result of the relative decrease in the agricultural population, the demand for the increased output of finished manufactured goods was sustained by other consumers with the aid of installment buying, favorable balance of trade, and speculative money incomes. Since the removal of the artificial supports of the market for manufactured goods, it is evident now that business would be less depressed if the farmers had more purchasing power.

Little importance attaches to the reparations and inter-Allied debt payments as a direct contributing cause of the present depression in the United States. We, in this country, developed the forces which produced the depression at a time when the reparations and the inter-Allied debt problems were as acute as they were in 1929. It seems a sound opinion that the present world-wide depression was produced in the United States, and, in so far as business has continued to become more depressed in the European nations, these nations have been adversely affected by what has developed in this country.

I agree with those who hold that both individual prices and the system of prices have lost some of the elasticity they used to have, and that this change has contributed to our present difficulties. The large business enterprises, particularly in the fields of mining, manufacturing and trade, through monopolies, cartels, and trade associations have been able in great measure to hold the prices of their products at relatively stable points in the face of an increasing output and lower costs. The farmers, on the other hand, partly because of the lack of joint ability to control output and the marketing of their products, have little power to hold up the prices of their products. Producers' control of the prices of one class of products and the lack of control by producers of another class of products have thrown the price system out of adjustment and have caused an unbalanced development of industry. This development has brought about a temporary break-down in the producers' control of the prices of manufactured goods.

Professor Joseph Schumpeter of Harvard does not contend that the high rate of wages contributed to the bringing about of the depression, but he does believe that the present high rate of wages retards the readjustments necessary for recovery. I believe that if the total amount of money paid out as wages from 1922 to 1929 had increased in proportion to the increase in value of the goods produced during that period, or if prices had generally followed the lead of declining costs, we should have had today only a very mild business depression, or none at all, instead of the very severe one we now have. If such had been the case, profits during the expansion period would have been less, production would not have increased as rapidly as it did, the stock market boom (based on higher profits and fed on bank credit) would not have occurred, and we should not have had much credit inflation. Installment buying would not have been as great, nor would the balance of foreign trade have been as large; but the home demand for consumers' goods would have been supported by actual money received rather than by artificial means.

There are many difficulties in the way of recovery from the present depression. I must say that I do not believe that high wages is one of these difficulties. I do not agree that the present widespread unemployment situation would be relieved materially by lowering wages. The larger part of the present unemployment is due to the closing down of industry which is due to the excess of goods in the markets, which in turn is due to the shortage of purchasing power of American consumers.

NECESSARY ECONOMIC CHANGES IN THE UNITED STATES

Modern capitalism is now out of its babyhood; it has reached the adolescent stage of growth. It was born less than two hundred years ago with the factory system when goods began to be produced for the market on a large scale. Modern capitalism was, of course, built upon the older institutions of private ownership of property and freedom of contract; it grew out of the domestic system of production where a price system was already in use. With the coming of automatic machinery, industrial society turned toward mass production and the seeking of large profits. Under this system we have learned to master the forces of nature sufficiently to increase man's productive power many times over his power under the old domestic economic system. The pursuit of profits was the underlying incentive which brought into action the forces which increased our power of production. From the standpoint of production of economic goods and services, we have today, the most effective industrial system the world has ever seen.

But in this system one outstanding weakness is now apparent. We have failed to develop effective methods of the distribution of money income to the mass of consumers. The money income received by consumers is not sufficiently large to enable them to purchase at prevailing prices the consumers' goods and services which our economic system produces. This outstanding weakness is a result largely of the desire for high profits on the part of managers.

* * *

In short, our outstanding economic problems today are: first, the increase in the purchasing power (or income) of consumers; second, the increase of jobs for laborers; and third, the direction or control of industrial development in such a manner that certain industries will not be overdeveloped.

The only way to increase substantially consumers' purchasing power is to increase the percentage of the national money income which goes to laborers as salaries and wages, and to decrease the percentage of it which goes to property owners as profits, interest, rentals, etc. In order to bring about this result, it will be necessary to increase the relative purchasing power of wage earners and to decrease the relative purchasing power of receivers of profits, interest, royalties, etc. This result may be brought about in part by decreasing the prices of commodities without at the same time decreasing the wage scale. To the extent to which prices at present are falling faster than wages, this result is now being accomplished. Again, the increase in the purchasing power of consumers may be brought about an increase in the daily wage scale, provided prices are not allowed to increase at the same time. Such a change in our national wage scale will necessarily reduce the rate of profits.

It is evident that putting into effect such a change in the distribution of the national money income would result in an immediate decrease in the capital values which have been built up, and would slow down the future accumulation of money savings and of new physical capital. According to our traditional way of thinking, such a result would prove injurious to our future economic progress, because capital would be discouraged and future savings would be inadequate to supply the necessary new capital. This traditional point of view is based on the theory that society must do everything it can to protect and promote the interest of capital in order that society may secure enough new capital to develop the necessary new industries and to expand the old ones. Whatever merit this theory may have had in the past, certainly it has little or no merit today in the face of the present situation with reference to the surplus supply of physical capital.

* * *

In so far as we have a general overproduction situation in industry in the United States, it was brought about by diverting too large a percentage of the national money income to making new capital investments and too small a percentage of the national money income to purchasing finished consumers' goods. This could happen only where profits have been too high and real wages too low, or where prices have not been adjusted to the lower cost of production during periods of economic progress. [Theoretically, competition should lower prices and reduce profits during periods of economic progress. But because of trade association agreements and other monopolistic price-control measures in operation from 1922 to 1929, big business kept prices from being lowered as rapidly as was the cost of production. Big have had, and in the future they are

business was able to hold prices up through agreements largely because of the enormous favorable balance of trade (financed by credit) and the increase in installment buying during the period 1922–29.] Again, because of the displacement of labor by automatic machinery from 1922 to 1929, the surplus of labor created kept real wages from increasing as rapidly as did profits.

The days of an artificially financed large favorable balance of trade are gone. In the near future our favorable balance of trade is likely to become quite small or to disappear. Installment buying in the United States is not likely to increase in the future; it may decrease. These two artificial forces have spent their power to hold up prices. Through a proper regulation of trade associations and other monopolistic control activities by big business, competition will force prices to respond to changes in the cost of production. The lowering of prices and profits will result in the increase of real wages. Thus competition, when given a chance, will bring about a more equitable distribution of the money income of the nation.

Recently several writers have advocated the organization of a national planning committee to lay out comprehensive plans whereby the nation's industries would be directed toward a balanced development so that there would be no general overproduction and no special overproduction. It is possible that the special overproduction problem might be aided by special national committees dealing with particular industries. But the position is taken here that the general overproduction problem could not be solved by a national planning committee made up of representatives of various industries.

Representatives of industry in the past likely to have, an acquisitive point of view. With few if any exceptions, such representatives who were with the federal government during the [First] World War were able to think and act only in terms of immediate profits to their industries. Few "dollar-a-year men" were able to think in terms of public welfare even in war time. The accepted method of securing immediate profits is to raise prices or keep prices up and lower the cost of production. It is feared that a national planning committee made up of representatives of industry would be able to think of their problem only in terms of the assurance of profits to their respective industries; as a rule, few such representatives are able to think in terms of the general welfare. Plans which would be brought forth by a committee with the acquisitive point of view would be quite similar to the tariff plan of Mr. Grundy and his Pennsylvania cohorts. This tariff plan appears to have been based on the principle that each industry should get all the protection it can, and in doing so it should support the policies of other industries in doing the same thing. The policies of such a planning committee would result in further maldistribution of the proceeds of industry and greater general overproduction (or underconsumption), in so far as its activities would affect the development of industry.

* * *

LEGISLATION TO PREVENT RECURRENCE OF A DEPRESSION

In order to put into effect the necessary change in the distribution of our national money income, our business leaders must realize that it will be possible to operate our economic system in the future only under conditions of a reasonable rate of profits; they must be willing either to pay higher wages or to accept relatively lower prices for their products. To create the necessary number of jobs, they must put into effect shorter hours for laborers. The national government can also do much, through legislation and administrative policies, to bring about the necessary changes in the distribution of the national money income. Such legislation should be along the following lines:

1. Revision of federal anti-trust acts: The anti-trust acts should be strengthened rather than abolished. We are now permitting too many trade associations to hold up prices by regulating output. These activities should be curbed by more stringent federal regulation. Technological progress has not been held back by federal anti-trust laws, nor has mass production been retarded by them. These laws have prevented the formation of some industrial combinations which would have resulted in higher prices, higher profits, and greater inflation of the securities of the particular companies.

* * *

A certain amount of coöperation between competitors is desirable, but there should be a federal law regulating the activities of trade associations. This law should require the Federal Trade Commission to regulate and supervise the activities of trade associations. The law should state specifically the kind of activities which would be unlawful for the trade associations to participate in, *i.e.*, such as price agreements, agreements to limit output in order to raise prices, etc. The law regulating trade associations should provide that representatives of the laborers as well as the employers shall have membership in these associations. Meetings of such associations should be attended by representatives of the Federal Trade Commission, and a record of their activities should be kept by the Federal Trade Commission as public documents.

Franklin D. Roosevelt: PLANS FOR RECOVERY

During the political conflict and economic innovation in the earlier New Deal period of 1933–37, there was a measure of economic recovery. When the downturn of 1937–38 interrupted the economy's slow progress toward recovery, President Roosevelt turned to the "underconsumption-overproduction" theory for an explanation. In April 1938, in the following "Fireside Chat," one of his intimate radio talks with the people, Roosevelt interpreted the setback in underconsumptionist terms and described his proposals to counter it.

FIVE months have gone by since I last spoke to the people of the Nation about the state of the Nation.

I had hoped to be able to defer this talk until next week because, as we all know, this is Holy Week. But what I want to say to you, the people of the country, is of such immediate need and relates so closely the lives of human beings and the prevention of human suffering that I have felt that there should be no delay. In this decision I have been strengthened by the thought that by speaking tonight there may be greater peace of mind and the hope of Easter may be more real at firesides everywhere, and that it is not inappropriate to encourage peace when so many of us are thinking of the Prince of Peace.

Five years ago we faced a very serious problem of economic and social recovery. For four and a half years that recovery proceeded apace. It is only in the past seven months that it has received a visible setback.

And it is only within the past two months, as we have waited patiently to see whether the forces of business itself would counteract it, that it has become apparent that government itself can no longer safely fail to take aggressive government steps to meet it.

This recession has not returned us to the disasters and suffering of the beginning of 1933. Your money in the bank is safe; farmers are no longer in deep distress and have greater purchasing power; dangers of security speculation have been minimized; national income is almost 50 per cent higher than in 1932; and government has an established and accepted responsibility for relief.

But I know that many of you have lost your jobs or have seen your friends or members of your families lose their jobs, and I do not propose that the government shall pretend not to see these things. I know that the effect of our present difficulties has been uneven; that they have affected some groups and some localities seriously, but that they have been scarcely felt in others. But I conceive the first duty of government is to protect the economic welfare of all the people in all sections and in all groups. I said in my message opening the last session of Congress that if private enterprise did not provide jobs this spring, government would take up the slack — that I would not let the people down. We have all learned the lesson that government cannot afford to wait until it has lost the power to act.

Therefore, I have sent a message of far-reaching importance to the Congress. I want to read to you tonight certain

From The Fireside Chat of April 14, 1938, in Samuel I. Rosenmann (comp.), *The Public Papers and Addresses of Franklin D. Roosevelt* (New York: Macmillan, 1941), Vol. VII, pp. 236–48.

passages from that message, and to talk with you about them.

In that message I analyzed the causes of the collapse of 1929 in these words: "overspeculation in and overproduction of practically every article or instrument used by man . . . millions of people had been put to work, but the products of their hands had exceeded the purchasing power of their pocketbooks. . . . Under the inexorable law of supply and demand, supplies so overran demand which would pay that production was compelled to stop. Unemployment and closed factories resulted. Hence the tragic years from 1929 to 1933."

I pointed out to the Congress that the national income — not the Government's income, but the total of the income of all the individual citizens and families of the United States — every farmer, every worker, every banker, every professional man and every person who lived on income derived from investments — that national income amounted, in the year 1929, to eighty-one billion dollars. By 1932 this had fallen to thirty-eight billion dollars. Gradually, and up to a few months ago, it had risen to a total of sixty-eight billion dollars — a pretty good come-back from the low point.

I then said this to the Congress:

"But the very vigor of the recovery in both durable goods and consumers' goods brought into the picture early in 1937 certain highly undesirable practices, which were in large part responsible for the economic decline which began in the later months of that year. Again production outran the ability to buy.

"There were many reasons for this overproduction. One was fear — fear of war abroad, fear of inflation, fear of nationwide strikes. None of these fears has been borne out.

". . . Production in many important lines of goods outran the ability of the public to purchase them. For example, through the winter and spring of 1937 cotton factories in hundreds of cases were running on a three-shift basis, piling up cotton goods in the factory and in the hands of middle men and retailers. For example, also, automobile manufacturers not only turned out a normal increase of finished cars, but encouraged the normal increase to run into abnormal figures, using every known method to push their sales. This meant, of course, that the steel mills of the Nation ran on a twenty-four hour basis, and the tire companies and cotton factories speeded up to meet the same type of abnormally stimulated demand. The buying power of the Nation lagged behind.

"Thus by the autumn of 1937 the Nation again had stocks on hand which the consuming public could not buy because the purchasing power of the consuming public had not kept pace with the production.

"During the same period . . . the prices of many vital products had risen faster than was warranted. . . . In the case of many commodities the price to the consumer was raised well above the inflationary boom prices of 1929. In many lines of goods and materials, prices got so high that buyers and builders ceased to buy or to build.

". . . The economic process of getting out the raw materials, putting them through the manufacturing and finishing processes, selling them to the retailers, selling them to the consumer, and finally using them got completely out of balance.

". . . The laying off of workers came upon us last autumn and has been continuing at such a pace ever since that all of us, Government and banking and business and workers, and those faced with destitution, recognize the need for action."

All of this I said to the Congress today and I repeat it to you, the people of the country, tonight.

I went on to point out to the Senate and the House of Representatives that all the energies of government and business must be directed to increasing the national income, to putting more people into private jobs, to giving security and a feeling of security to all people in all walks of life.

I am constantly thinking of all our people — unemployed and employed alike — of their human problems of food and clothing and homes and education and health and old age. You and I agree that security is our greatest need; the chance to work, the opportunity of making a reasonable profit in our business — whether it be a very small business or a larger one — the possibility of selling our farm products for enough money for our families to live on decently. I know these are the things that decide the well-being of all our people.

Therefore, I am determined to do all in my power to help you attain that security, and because I know that the people themselves have a deep conviction that secure prosperity of that kind cannot be a lasting one except on a basis of business fair dealing and a basis where all from top to bottom share in prosperity, I repeated to the Congress today that neither it nor the Chief Executive can afford "to weaken or destroy great reforms which, during the past five years, have been effected on behalf of the American people. In our rehabilitation of the banking structure and of agriculture, in our provisions for adequate and cheaper credit for all types of business, in our acceptance of national responsibility for unemployment relief,

in our strengthening of the credit of state and local government, in our encouragement of housing, slum clearance and home ownership, in our supervision of stock exchanges and public utility holding companies and the issuance of new securities, in our provision for social security, the electorate of America wants no backward steps taken.

"We have recognized the right of labor to free organization, to collective bargaining; and machinery for the handling of labor relations is now in existence. The principles are established even though we can all admit that, through the evolution of time, administration and practices can be improved. Such improvement can come about most quickly and most peacefully through sincere efforts to understand and assist on the part of labor leaders and employers alike. . . ."

I came to the conclusion that the present-day problem calls for action both by the Government and by the people, that we suffer primarily from a failure of consumer demand because of lack of buying power. It is up to us to create an economic upturn.

"How and where can and should the Government help to start an upward spiral?"

I went on to propose three groups of measures and I will summarize the recommendations.

First, I asked for certain appropriations which are intended to keep the Government expenditures for work relief and similar purposes during the coming fiscal year at the same rate of expenditure as at present. That includes additional money for the Works Progress Administration; additional funds for the Farm Security Administration; additional allotments for the National Youth Administration, and more money for the

Civilian Conservation Corps, in order that it can maintain the existing number of camps now in operation.

These appropriations, made necessary by increased unemployment, will cost about a billion and a quarter more than the estimates which I sent to the Congress on the third of January.

Second, I told the Congress that the Administration proposes to make additional bank reserves available for the credit needs of the country. About one billion four hundred million dollars of gold now in the Treasury will be used to pay these additional expenses of the Government, and three-quarters of a billion dollars of additional credit will be made available to the banks by reducing the reserves now required by the Federal Reserve Board.

These two steps, taking care of relief needs and adding to bank credits, are in our judgment insufficient by themselves to start the Nation on a sustained upward movement.

Therefore, I came to the third kind of Government action which I consider to be vital. I said to the Congress:

"You and I cannot afford to equip ourselves with two rounds of ammunition where three rounds are necessary. If we stop at relief and credit, we may find ourselves without ammunition before the enemy is routed. If we are fully equipped with the third round of ammunition, we stand to win the battle against adversity."

The third proposal is to make definite additions to the purchasing power of the Nation by providing new work over and above the continuing of the old work.

First, to enable the United States Housing Authority to undertake the immediate construction of about three hundred million dollars of additional slum clearance projects.

Second, to renew a public works program by starting as quickly as possible about one billion dollars worth of needed permanent public improvements in states, counties and cities.

Third, to add one hundred million dollars to the estimate for federal aid highways in excess of the amount I recommended in January.

Fourth, to add thirty-seven million dollars over and above the former estimate of sixty-three million dollars for flood control and reclamation.

Fifth, to add twenty-five million dollars additional for federal buildings in various parts of the country.

In recommending this program I am thinking not only of the immediate economic needs of the people of the Nation, but also of their personal liberties — the most precious possession of all Americans. I am thinking of our democracy and of the recent trend in other parts of the world away from the democratic ideal.

Democracy has disappeared in several other great nations — not because the people of those nations disliked democracy, but because they had grown tired of unemployment and insecurity, of seeing their children hungry while they sat helpless in the face of government confusion and government weakness through lack of leadership in government. Finally, in desperation, they chose to sacrifice liberty in the hope of getting something to eat. We in America know that our own democratic institutions can be preserved and made to work. But in order to preserve them we need to act together, to meet the problems of the Nation boldly, and to prove that the practical operation of democratic government is equal to the task of protecting the security of the people.

Not only our future economic soundness but the very soundness of our demo-cratic institutions depends on the deter-mination of our Government to give employment to idle men. The people of America are in agreement in defending their liberties at any cost, and the first line of that defense lies in the protection of economic security. Your Government, seeking to protect democracy, must prove that Government is stronger than the forces of business depression.

History proves that dictatorships do not grow out of strong and successful governments, but out of weak and help-less ones. If by democratic methods people get a government strong enough to protect them from fear and starvation, their democracy succeeds; but if they do not, they grow impatient. Therefore, the only sure bulwark of continuing liberty is a government strong enough to pro-tect the interests of the people, and a people strong enough and well enough informed to maintain its sovereign con-trol over its government.

We are a rich Nation; we can afford to pay for security and prosperity with-out having to sacrifice our liberties in the bargain.

In the first century of our republic we were short of capital, short of workers and short of industrial production; but we were rich in free land, free timber and free mineral wealth. The Federal Government rightly assumed the duty of promoting business and relieving depres-sion by giving subsidies of land and other resources.

Thus, from our earliest days we have had a tradition of substantial govern-ment help to our system of private enter-prise. But today the government no longer has vast tracts of rich land to give away and we have discovered that we must spend large sums to conserve our land from further erosion and our forests

from further depletion. The situation is also very different from the old days, be-cause now we have plenty of capital, banks and insurance companies loaded with idle money; plenty of industrial productive capacity and several millions of workers looking for jobs. It is follow-ing tradition as well as necessity, if Gov-ernment strives to put idle money and idle men to work, to increase our public wealth and to build up the health and strength of the people — and to help our system of private enterprise to function.

It is going to cost something to get out of this recession this way, but the profit of getting out of it will pay for the cost several times over. Lost working time is lost money. Every day that a workman is unemployed, or a machine is unused, or a business organization is marking time, is a loss to the Nation. Because of idle men and idle machines this Nation lost one hundred billion dollars between 1929 and the spring of 1933. This year you, the people of this country, are mak-ing about twelve billion dollars less than last year.

If you think back to the experiences of the early years of this Administration you will remember the doubts and fears ex-pressed about the rising expenses of Gov-ernment. But to the surprise of the doubters, as we proceeded to carry on the program which included Public Works and Work Relief, the country grew richer instead of poorer.

It is worthwhile to remember that the annual national people's income was thirty billion dollars more in 1937 than in 1932. It is true that the national debt increased sixteen billion dollars, but re-member that in this increase must be included several billion dollars worth of assets which eventually will reduce that debt and that many billion dollars of per-manent public improvements — schools, roads, bridges, tunnels, public buildings, parks and a host of other things — meet your eye in every one of the thirty one hundred counties in the United States.

No doubt you will be told that the Government spending program of the past five years did not cause the increase in our national income. They will tell you that business revived because of private spending and investment. That is true in part, for the Government spent only a small part of the total. But Government spending acted as a trigger to set off private activity. That is why the total addition to our national production and national income has been so much greater than the contribution of the Government itself.

In pursuance of that thought I said to the Congress today: "I want to make it clear that we do not believe that we can get an adequate rise in national income merely by investing, lending or spending public funds. It is essential in our economy that private funds be put to work

and all of us recognize that such funds are entitled to a fair profit."

As national income rises, "let us not forget that Government expenditures will go down and Government tax receipts will go up."

The Government contribution of land that we once made to business was the land of all the people. And the Government contribution of money which we now make to business ultimately comes out of the labor of all the people. It is, therefore, only sound morality, as well as a sound distribution of buying power, that the benefits of the prosperity coming from this use of the money of all the people should be distributed among all the people — at the bottom as well as at the top. Consequently I am again expressing my hope that the Congress will enact at this session a wage and hour bill putting a floor under industrial wages and a limit on working hours — to ensure a better distribution of our prosperity, a better distribution of available work, and a sounder distribution of buying power.

Gardiner C. Means: INFLEXIBLE PRICES AND THEIR EFFECT

In collaboration with Adolf A. Berle, Jr., Gardiner Means published in 1932 a striking and greatly influential work, The Modern Corporation and Private Property, which stressed the high concentration of economic power in the modern business system. During succeeding years Means pursued the implications of this concentration and the effects of the price rigidity which he maintained that it caused. The essay reproduced below was read originally as a paper in December 1934 at the annual meeting of the American Statistical Association.

IN TRADITIONAL economic writings dealing with the economy as a whole, it is usually assumed that prices are highly flexible and that economic adjustment is brought about through price changes. We are going to examine in-

From Gardiner C. Means, "Price Inflexibility and the Requirements of a Stabilizing Monetary Policy," *Journal of the American Statistical Association*, Vol. XXX, 190 (June 1935), pp. 401–13. Reprinted by permission of the publishers and of the author.

flexible prices. In doing so, I want to draw a sharp distinction between traditional market prices and what I will call administered prices. By market prices, I mean prices that are made *in* the market as the result of the interaction of buyers and sellers as are the prices of wheat and cotton.

Administered prices are essentially different. By an administered price I mean one which is set by administrative action and held constant for a period of time. We have an administered price when a company maintains a posted price at which it will make sales. Very many of our wholesale prices are administered and the great body of retail prices are administered rather than market prices, for many wholesalers and most retailers set their price for a period of time and the buyers can buy or not buy at the price set. For administered prices, the price is rigid, at least for a period of time, and sales fluctuate with the demand at the rigid price.

This distinction between market prices and administered prices is not the old distinction between competitive prices and monopoly prices. In many competitive industries such as the automobile industry prices are made administratively and held for fairly long periods of time. On the other hand, it is conceivable that, in a monopolized industry, the product might be turned out according to some fixed production schedule and sold for what it would bring in the market regardless of price. Thus, in the first case we would have administered prices in a competitive industry and in the second case, market prices in a monopolized industry. In general, however, monopolized industries have administered prices though the opposite is not true. Administered prices are also to be found in a great many highly competitive industries.

The importance of these administered prices is clear if we study the prices of the separate commodities entering into the Bureau of Labor Statistics wholesale price index to discover the frequency of price change for each separate item. Examination of the monthly figures between 1926 and 1933 shows that some items did not change a single time in eight years. Other items changed in price every single month in the period. A great many items fell between the two extremes. . . .

But while these prices are inflexible, since they do not change *frequently,* are they also inflexible in that they show little amplitude of price change? [Available data] shows clearly that frequency of price change and magnitude of price change in the depression have gone together. . . .The items which changed frequently in price showed a large drop during the depression while those having a low frequency of change tended to drop little in price.

A warning must be issued against the easy assumption that a failure of a price to come down reflects an inelastic demand for the commodity. It is frequently pointed out that in most of the industries in which prices have not dropped, a lowering of price would not increase sales sufficiently to justify the individual firm in revising its administered price downward. This is usually taken as evidence of an inelastic demand. It might equally indicate that the individual firm had such a large production in relation to the whole market that a lowered price on its current restricted output would more than counterbalance any gain from increased sales at the lower price. It is well known that the demands for automobiles and agricultural implements are much more elastic than those of food and shoes. Yet the latter fell in price while production was curtailed in the former. We must look elsewhere than to the inelasticity of demand to understand inflexible prices.

What is the meaning of these inflexible administered prices? . . . One must conclude that inflexible administered prices are a major factor in our economy. This conclusion is heightened when we add the relative inflexibility of railroad and utility rates, of salaries and often of labor rates, of many commercial loan rates, and of many government services. We have long accepted inflexible administered prices in the government and utility fields though we have never taken full account of their effect on the economy as a whole. But to find inflexible prices a dominant factor in that part of our economy which has been regarded as competitive and in which prices have been assumed to be flexible must give the basis for most serious thought.

The most immediate significance of these inflexible prices lies in their disruptive effect on the functioning of our economy. We have always relied in the past on the automatic balancing of economic activity through price changes. This is all right where prices are flexible, since a general drop in demand such as occurred in the depression would result in a drop in prices and maintained production. If all prices had been flexible it is doubtful if we would have had a serious depression after the stock crash of 1929. Where prices are rigid, however, a general drop in demand has quite different and most disastrous results. Instead of producing lower prices, the drop in demand produces a drop in sales and in production. Workers and machines are thrown out of use and both owners and workers have less to spend, thus amplifying the original drop in demand. In this manner, rigid prices can expand an

initial small fluctuation of industrial activity into a cataclysmic depression.

The whole different reaction of flexible market prices and inflexible administered prices is clearly brought out in Charts II and IV.[1] Chart III shows the changes in prices and production for agriculture as a whole during the depression. Not until the control program in 1933 was there any significant drop in agricultural production. Practically the whole impact of falling demand worked itself out in falling prices. Chart IV shows the opposite development for agricultural implements — though in a somewhat exaggerated form because of small price concessions not easily reflected in the index.

A similar story is told when we examine particular industries. Thus, for ten major industries the drop in prices and production from 1929 to the spring of 1933 were approximately as follows:

	Per cent Drop in Prices	Per cent Drop in Production
Agricultural Implements	6	80
Motor Vehicles	16	80
Cement	18	65
Iron and Steel	20	83
Auto Tires	33	70
Textile Products	45	30
Food Products	49	14
Leather	50	20
Petroleum	56	20
Agricultural Commodities	63	6

One can make the broad generalization, having of course many exceptions, that for industries in which prices dropped most during the depression, production tended to drop least while for those in which prices were maintained the drop in production was usually greatest.

But such an analysis only gives us the

[1] The charts referred to here and elsewhere in the text have been omitted since the author's meaning is readily evident without them. [Editor's note.]

disrupting effect of inflexible administered prices, not their basic significance.
This can be obtained only by going back
a little in our history and envisaging the
process of economic concentration which
has been under way during the last century. It has been traditional to say that
economic activity is coordinated primarily through the buying and selling in the
market; that the independent action of
separate individuals and firms is brought
together in a more or less unified whole
by the price mechanism and the market
place. But the last century has seen a
steadily increasing shift from market
coordination to administrative coordination. Gradually, as our great corporations have been built up, more and more
of the coordination of individual economic action has been brought about
administratively. In the Steel Corporation the activity of over two hundred
thousand men has been coordinated and
made to mesh into a great producing
organization. In 1932 more than half the
assets of all manufacturing companies
were held by 200 great corporations.

As a result of this shift from market to
administration, the area of coordination
remaining to the market has been greatly
reduced while the increased bargaining
power of the big administrative units has
induced the counter concentration in the
form of cooperative bargaining organization, farm cooperatives, labor unions and
to a small extent consumer cooperatives,
thus reducing the number of separate
units interacting through the market.

This shift from market to administrative coordination has carried administration into the market itself. Prices have
become problems of administration. General Motors goes through a long process
in deciding what prices to set. Indeed
as we go from the atomistic to the concentrated industries we find more admin-

istered prices and the administered prices
becoming more rigid. In spite of many
exceptions, the more concentrated the
industry in relation to its market, the
more inflexible do prices become. Of
course, in the monopolized industries like
pig aluminum and nickel, rigid prices are
to be expected. But even in the concentrated but competitive industries such as
automobiles, the rigidity of prices is evident while in the dispersed industries
like farming, garment making, standard
cotton manufacturing, etc., prices are
extremely flexible. Though no study has
yet been made which conclusively establishes this correlation between price
rigidity and concentration, preliminary
studies clearly indicate its existence.
Furthermore, this correlation is to be expected on theoretical grounds. When the
number of producers supplying a market
has been reduced to the point where an
individual firm has to take into account
the effect on prices of its own changes in
production, then it will usually be to the
interest of the individual firm to meet a
declining demand primarily with a reduction in production and only second-
arily with a decline in price. It seems
clear that concentration has been a major,
though undoubtedly not the only, factor
in producing rigid administered prices.
Thus, in their general significance these
rigid prices reflect the long progress of
economic concentration and appear to be
an internal part of modern industrial organization resting on modern technology.

If we accept the preceding analysis and
the conclusion (1) that inflexible administered prices are a major factor in our
economy, (2) that they constitute a serious impediment to balanced economic
functioning, and (3) that they result primarily from and are inherent in economic
concentration and modern industrial organization, then we are indeed faced

with a serious problem. To me this presents the major problem of the present day. Unless we would accept a poorly functioning economy, one that gets worse with further concentration, the conflict between inflexible prices and a smoothly functioning economy must be resolved.

How can this conflict be resolved? Two essentially different paths lie open to us. We might reverse the long-time process of concentration by breaking up concentrated administrative coordination to the point that largely eliminates inflexible prices. Or we might accept inflexible prices as inherent in our modern economy and build our economic institutions around them in such a manner that inflexible administered prices will cease to be a disrupting factor.

If we would follow the first road toward breaking up large scale enterprise so as to produce flexible market prices, it would almost certainly mean a lower material standard of living than modern technology and modern industrial organization make possible. Few who advocate such a course seem to realize the extent to which the pulverizing process would have to go in order to make prices really flexible. Would not such a disruption of modern industrial organization be a wasteful and retrograde step? Is there no satisfactory alternative? What of the second road — the acceptance of inflexible prices where necessary and the building of economic institutions such that rigid prices and all that lie behind them cease to be a disrupting factor? Can such a road be followed without destroying democratic institutions? I believe not only that social forces will take us along the second road whether we like it or not, but that the second road can be followed without destroying our democracy.

If we accept modern industrial organization and the inflexible administered prices which appear to be inherent in it, and at the same time would retain democracy, then we have a problem of supplementing the market to the point where the economy as a whole functions effectively. In this paper I am only going into the essentials of the monetary policy dictated by inflexible prices. But monetary policy can be only one of the means for regaining or maintaining a properly functioning economy and in order that it may be considered in its proper perspective I shall outline what appear to me to be the major essentials for maintaining the effective functioning of an economy dominated by great corporate enterprises and inflexible prices.

First, all pressure for making for a *general revision* of prices either upward or downward would have to be eliminated since any development requiring a general change in the inflexible prices would actually result in a change in production and economic unbalance. This means that a monetary policy would have to be adopted which aimed to keep the flexible prices *as a group* approximately in line with inflexible prices *as a group,* and that a mechanism for the adjustment of international trade balances through *general changes* in price levels would have to be replaced.

Second, new techniques of control would have to be developed for establishing the necessary elements of industrial policy so that the self-interest of individuals working through the market but limited by the framework of policy established would tend to produce the optimum use of human and material resources.

Finally, violent dislocations in the flow of savings into capital goods would have to be minimized.

These lines requiring institutional development are blocked out here in order that the remainder of this paper dealing with money will not stand isolated from the structural outline of the future economy into which it would have to fit. I hope at a later time to sketch in more detail the character of the institutions which could be developed to canalize economic activity and individual initiative into paths which would make for effective economic functioning and the optimum use of human and material resources.

So far as monetary policy alone is concerned, what are the requirements of such a policy in the presence of inflexible prices and how would it differ from monetary policy in an economy containing only flexible prices? If all prices were perfectly flexible, as is so often assumed in monetary discussions, the main problem of policy would be concentrated on making the monetary medium — currency and deposits — as safe and liquid as possible. There would be no problem of getting the "right amount" of monetary medium in the economy. Whatever the amount, prices would presumably adjust and changes either in volume of money or in money needs would only result in changes in the general level of prices, not in serious changes in *price relationships*. Changes in the amount of money in circulation or in need for money would not disrupt the economy, though they might change the relationships between debtor and creditor.

Inflexible prices introduce a new element and established the need for furnishing the *"right amount"* of monetary medium as well as need for making it safe and liquid. This can clearly be seen by considering the effect of a reduction in the money supply. Assume that the price structure was in balance at the outset. Then let the volume of money — deposits and currency — be reduced with no corresponding reduction in the need for money. It is usually assumed, and I believe correctly, that the first effect would be a drop in demand for goods and services more or less all along the line. In a flexible priced economy a lower level of prices would presumably result. In an economy dominated by inflexible prices, the drop in demand would produce a drop in price among the flexible prices and a drop in sales, in production and in employment of men and machines in the rigid-priced industries. Thus, a reduction of the money volume could throw the latter economy into serious and continuing depression.

Similarly, if the volume of money were to remain constant while the community's need for money to support the existing price structure increased, the presence of the rigid-priced industries would bring about falling industrial activity and depression. If, for instance, the stock-market crash in 1929 made the business community uncertain as to what was to follow and as a result, individual business men tried to make their assets more liquid — i.e., shifted from inventories to money and from less liquid to more liquid securities and to money, — we would have had an increased demand for money and a smaller demand for goods and securities. If an increased supply of money were not forthcoming, the effect on prices and production would be the same as if there had been an actual reduction in the volume of money. Perhaps such a development partly explains the depression.

Let us trace the downward sweep of prices during the depression and their subsequent upswing. Chart V shows price indexes for ten separate groups of commodities selected and arranged according to increasing *frequency* of price change. It does not use the customary arrangement of indexes with time running along the horizontal axis. Rather, time is represented by the successive lines on the chart and the price relatives for different commodity groups are arranged along the horizontal axis according to increasing frequency of price change. At the left, are the commodity groups made up of items that changed infrequently in price. At the right are the commodity groups made up of items which changed price frequently. Each group is represented by a series of dots indicating the level of prices at successive dates with the 1929 prices as 100. For the inflexible group I, prices remained constant. For intermediate groups the successive prices fell to an intermediate degree. Each line on the chart ties together the price relatives of the ten different commodity groups at one particular date. The progress of the depression is shown by the general swing down of the successive lines. The whole price structure pivoted around the rigid prices. The relative uniformity of the swing down should be noted for it seems to reflect a very real set of basic price relationships. If we had exactly similar indexes for production for each group of items the picture of the depression would be exactly reversed. We would find production reduced most at the rigid end of the scale and least at the flexible end. The whole structure of *production* would be shown to have pivoted around the flexible-priced commodities. Indeed, one might properly describe the whole depression as a general dropping of prices at the flexible end of the price scale and a dropping of production at the rigid end with intermediate effects between. The reverse process has been taking place during the last year and a half, but in a more spasmodic fashion as is shown in the lower part of Chart V.

The adoption of a policy which would keep flexible prices in line with the in-flexible prices and flexible production in line with inflexible production would require that at all times the varying demand for liquidity on the part of individuals be met, insofar as that is possible, through the monetary system. Back in 1913, we reorganized our banking system so as to eliminate, so far as possible, the panic conditions which result from the demand for the extreme liquidity involved in gold hoarding such as produced the gold panic of 1907. Under the Federal Reserve System, the efforts of individual banks to convert their assets into the most liquid asset, bank reserves, can be met by creating additional reserves. In a similar manner it would be necessary for economic stability that the demand on the part of individuals to become more liquid — to hold more of that most liquid asset, money, be met by increasing the money supply. Unless this were done the desire for increased liquidity would, in and of itself, bring action which would disrupt the economy so long as there was an important body of inflexible prices. To the extent that individuals or enterprises want to become more liquid, by increasing their money holdings and reducing their holdings of goods or securities, this desire must be met. The pools that will absorb money and hold it idle must be filled up if flexible prices are to be kept in line with the inflexible prices and the disrupting influence of the latter nullified. Likewise, to the extent that individuals and enterprises want to become less liquid — for instance, after crisis fear has subsided — then a stabilizing monetary policy calls for reduction of the money supply so as to reabsorb the money no longer held stagnant in idle pools. Such would be the monetary policy which would contribute most to economic stability in the presence of inflexible prices.

H. L. McCracken: TECHNOLOGICAL CHANGE, MONOPOLISTIC COMPETITION, AND UNEMPLOYMENT

One of the most significant economic treatises ever written by an American appeared in 1933 with the publication of Edward Chamberlin's The Theory of Monopolistic Competition. Traditionally, economists had conceptually divided the economy into two types of industries. Those industries with only one firm, or with one very dominant firm, constituted monopolies, while other industries were considered competitive. Chamberlin's theory entirely revolutionized this traditional view by persuasively arguing that, except for industries which contained so many competitors that no one producer had significant influence on pricing, the behavior of the industries composing the economy was "monopolistic." That is, the prices in most industries were maintained at as high a level as if the industries were simply monopolies.

The implication of Chamberlin's theory was that noncompetitive price-making was very extensive. In an essay of 1938 H. L. McCracken, then Professor of Economics at Louisiana State University, investigated the effect of monopolistic competition upon the economy's ability to expand to full employment, and found it a harmful one. McCracken's discussion, from which the following excerpt is taken, is an excellent example of the argumentation which led to and supported the reinvigoration of antitrust enforcement under Assistant Attorney General Thurman Arnold during the last stage of the New Deal in the late '30's.

THE FUNCTION OF PRICE IN A COMPETITIVE ORDER

ALL ECONOMISTS, regardless of the school of thought to which they may belong or assign themselves, probably agree that the major functions of price in a competitive order are those of control and coordination. Price is a part of the law of demand and supply. If price has gravitated to the point where demand and supply are thrown into equilibrium and then a dynamic factor enters in the form of an increased demand, it is the function of price to rise until demand and supply are again in adjustment. In the field of normal value if the cost of producing a reproducible good declines, price is expected to fall in harmony with reduced cost and establish a new equilibrium. Furthermore, this would undoubtedly happen if production and exchange took place in a frictionless economy marked by "free prices, with wages and other elements of production cost completely flexible, with labor and capital completely mobile."

THE NATURE OF MONOPOLISTIC COMPETITION

No one can look about upon the economic world in which we find ourselves without being keenly cognizant of the fact that we do not live in a frictionless world of free competition and flexible

From H. L. McCracken, "Monopolistic Competition and Business Fluctuations," *Southern Economic Journal*, Vol. V, 2 (October 1938), pp. 158–66, 177–78. Reprinted by permission of the *Southern Economic Journal*.

price. Our modern economy is marked by frictions of many types, by rigid prices administered by government or business organizations sufficiently unified and powerful to control supply and regulate price. As to the factors in production, land is immobile; large segments of capital are fixed and specialized; and much labor is incapable of transfer whether due to the possession of a specialized skill, to sentimental ties or to the lack of funds with which to effect a transfer. It is this relatively rigid world of frictions and inflexibility with which we have to live and which we are called upon to analyze.

Whereas one of the major functions of competition is to keep price related to cost, we all know that the major purpose of monopoly is to break the connection between cost and price. Monopoly is designed to "charge all the traffic will bear" regardless of cost. Where does monopolistic competition stand in this connection between pure competition and pure monopoly? . . .

It is [Chamberlin's] contention that where business men are far-sighted so that present decisions are made by forecasting the probable future effects of any price and production policy upon other producers in the same field then oligopoly will approximate the same supply and price as monopoly. . . .

Although this theory of monopolistic competition is relatively new, Chamberlin's contention is rapidly gaining recognition and acceptance. The major point in his argument is that we do not jump from monopoly price and output restriction as soon as two or more competitors enter the same field, but that the price and production pattern tends to resemble monopoly far more than competition until the number of producers in any given field becomes so large that no one cor-

poration or entrepreneur is large enough to have significance with respect to the whole.

If this theory of monopolistic competition is valid, then the presence in any field of a dominant corporation large enough to have significance tends to be destructive of competition and competitive price. Furthermore, oligopoly or any arrangement whereby a few large companies supply a given market will tend to restrict output or adjust supply to a maximum net revenue point not unlike monopoly even though there is no agreement or understanding among them.

The point of major significance involved in the distinction between competition and monopolistic competition is the technique utilized for purposes of control and coordination. As indicated above, competition tends toward capacity production and an equilibrium between demand and supply through flexible prices. Monopolistic competition tends to achieve equilibrium by holding prices relatively rigid and restricting the output to the demand which will be effective at the pre-determined price. Herein lies a matter of great significance. On the one hand, the controlling and coordinating force is a flexible price, and on the other, a flexible volume of production.

MONOPOLISTIC COMPETITION AND TECHNOLOGICAL CHANGE

The fear of technological unemployment is as old as the Industrial Revolution. In 1767, the neighbors of James Hargreaves organized a mob, broke into his home and demolished his "Spinning Jenny" because they had heard that it would do the work of eight spinsters. Indeed, Dame Rumor has it that they left the house shouting "Technological Unemployment." In 1816, the textile town of Nottingham was troubled by night raiders known as the "Luddites," who destroyed the machinery that was robbing the spinners and weavers of their jobs.

Yet, dynamic as was the period of the Industrial Revolution, yielding a continuous stream of new machines to supplant labor, the economic order absorbed them and met the adjustment with a minimum of suffering and unemployment. The logical explanation for the absorption of technological progress is well known. It runs about as follows: (1) Intelligent business men introduce machinery if and when it reduces cost. (2) If competition is effective, cost reduction is followed by price deduction. (3) If price falls, more goods are bought, particularly in fields characterized by a relatively elastic demand. (4) If more goods are bought, displaced men will have to be recalled to produce them. (5) If more goods are produced, more raw materials will be needed. (6) If machines do the work of men, men will have to make the machines.

The above logic proceeds from the hypothesis of effective competition. How is the picture altered when monopoly enters the field? As indicated above, the major purpose of monopoly is to break the connection between cost and price. Therefore, when a monopolistic industry introduces machinery or other labor-saving devices and thereby reduces cost there is no guarantee whatsoever that reduced cost will be followed by reduced price. But, if prices are not reduced the quantity demanded and consumed cannot increase; no additional raw materials are needed and none of the former workers are recalled to help supply a greater market. Thus, monopoly steps in to break the entire chain of events by which progress repairs itself. Furthermore, the same logic applies to monopolistic competition since it also tends toward monopoly price and adjusts supply to demand by control of output.

Although opinion may differ as to the extent and degree of monopolistic competition now obtaining, we may confidently conclude that "The more direct the connection between enhanced purchasing power and productive energy released by new techniques, the less the maladjustment and the more efficient the utilization of the new techniques. The less direct the connection, and the more diffused the transmission of new purchasing power to released productive energies, the greater and the more protracted are the resulting disturbances likely to be." In other words, abstract theory or the logic of cause and effect would teach one to expect that technological unemployment and business fluctuations resulting from the dynamics of change would be mild and unimportant if competition were prevalent and equilibrium sought by flexible price and capacity production; conversely, that technological unemployment and business fluctuations resulting from the dynamics of change would become increasingly severe, as business moved in the direction of monopolistic competition with prices relatively rigid and equilibrium sought by means of flexible production.

Although the entire nineteenth century was continuously and incessantly dynamic, with machinery and labor-saving devices following fast upon the heels of each other in all branches of trade and commerce, yet, jobs increased faster than population and a higher per cent of eligible workers was employed in 1900 than in 1800. Furthermore, according to Mills, this trend continued up to 1914 or the beginning of the World War. But for some reason or other the trend was reversed during the war with the result that progress did not repair itself nor the technologically displaced worker find re-employment during the prosperous decade of the twenties. . . . We find ourselves in agreement with Professor Kreps of Stanfard University, who says "The central fact that emerges is that over the 34-year period from 1899 to 1933, the productivity of the direct labor employed in the manufacturing industries had increased 130 per cent, 43 men in 1933 being able to produce as much as 100 men did in 1899.

"Who got the increased product? In the period from 1899 to 1914 the consumer, especially the farmer, mostly in the form of lower prices for manufactured goods. While output per worker increased 30 per cent, the real income of those engaged in manufacturing increased only 3 per cent per worker. The exchange value of manufacturers' services went down by amounts ranging from 12 to 23 per cent. Employment consequently increased, 700 new men being employed by manufacturing industries for every 100 men displaced by technological advance."

Quite the reverse was the case during the post-war period. Whereas, the productivity per worker increased even more — 43 per cent, as a matter of fact between 1919–1929 — real prices to the consumer fell very little. This was because the margin of profit between cost and sale price grew wider and wider. The period was marked "by an increase in the margin representing fabricational and distributional costs; . . . by low returns and deficient purchasing power of important classes of primary producers; . . . by high prices of articles intended for use in capital equipment; . . . by a plateau of high prices for finished goods intended for human consumption." In the existence of this plateau of high prices of goods ready for use "we have a very significant feature of the postwar decade. . . . It involves a transference of purchasing power to fabricators, a reduction in the purchasing power of primary producers and of those ultimate users (consumers and industrial users of equipment) who do not profit from the enlarged fabricational margin."

What was the result of this increasing margin between the cost and price of manufactured goods? What happens when the gains of technological improvements are not shared with farmers and city consumers in reduced prices? The answer is given by the National Bureau of Economic Research. "Quite the most important result was unemployment, only 91 men being employed in manufacturing for every 100 men displaced, even during the prosperous period from 1923 to 1929."

Why Technology Repaired itself before the War, but not After

Statistical evidence has been given to show that prior to the war reduced costs were passed on to consumers in reduced prices and that employment expanded with the introduction of machinery instead of contracting. After the war, reduced costs were not passed on to consumers, and employment did not expand but contracted as labor-saving devices were introduced. Here is a phenomenon greatly in need of explanation. The conclusion reached by Mills and those associated with him was that competition was fairly general before the war and prices quite flexible and responsive to changes in cost. Following the war, these conditions no longer obtained. The rise of "price regulation, monopolistic, and semi-monopolistic control, trade agreements, extensive valorization effort, — these and other influences tended to render price a less sensitive agency for the transmission of economic intelligence." ". . . Business conventions, monopolistic powers, legal restrictions, contractual obligations, . . . and rigid monetary charges tended to freeze great areas of the price system. It was these frictions that prevented the prompt and full utilization of technical improvements."

The same idea was stated in much more vigorous fashion by Harold G. Moulton, Director of the Brookings Institution.

The development of trade associations in the 1920's was systematically encouraged under the leadership of the United States Department of Commerce. Indeed 'stabilization' was one of the fundamental policies of the Hoover regime — the stabilization of prices being regarded as a means of preventing disorganization and hence as a key to stable production and permanent prosperity.

The evolution of industrial policy in recent times has thus served in substantial measure to prevent or impede the functioning of the competitive price mechanism. That is to say, over an ever-widening segment of the economic system the process of persistently expanding purchasing power by means of price reductions (as technological changes drive costs downward) has been checked. Thus one of the primary agencies of adjustment upon which the capitalistic system was supposed to rely has in substantial degree ceased to be operative.

As a result of this drive on the part of business men for stabilization through trade associations, and finally for outright repeal of anti-trust legislation, "The necessity of progressive price reductions as a means of expanding purchasing power and markets appears to have been forgotten, alike by business managers and economic statesmen. The conclusion is inescapable, however, that in so far as the effort to stabilize prices is effective

the broad distribution of income upon which continuous economic expansion depends is circumvented."

Let us now pause to make a few important observations in the light of the historical data just presented. First, the industrial system absorbed technological progress without serious difficulty before the war but has not since. Second, employment increased faster than population before the war and has not since. Third, competition was keener and more general with prices more flexible before the war than since. Fourth, reduced costs were passed on to the consumer in reduced prices to a greater degree before the war than since. Fifth, business fluctuations tended to be less violent and depressions less prolonged before the war than since. Is not one justified in concluding that we are dealing here with facts and phenomena causally related? Those associated with the National Bureau of Economic Research and the Brookings Institution, after extended research and analysis, have come to that conclusion and the present writer concurs in their opinion.

We are well aware that there are honest and able writers advising us to make our economic structure less competitive. There are pressure groups urging the relaxation of our anti-trust legislation. Yet, if logic may still be trusted, and if credence may be given to the evidence submitted by Mills and Moulton, then it would appear that "The Problem of Business Equilibration" is made vastly more difficult by the growth of business organizations with power to create sticky price structures and frozen price areas within the economic system; that equilibrium and capacity production would be more nearly approximated if competition were more general and more of the prices flexible; that our depressions would become shorter and less severe if we would turn our backs upon the monopolist's formula of "economic stabilization through price stabilization," and turn our faces toward the competitive formula of "stabilized production through price flexibility."

* * *

For these reasons, we believe that much of the discussion in recent years centering around flexible and inflexible prices has been largely irrelevant to the real problem involved. It is beside the point to argue that flexible prices are the "saints" and rigid prices the "sinners" or even vice versa. What really is relevant, in a dynamic era characterized by rapid and phenomenal reductions in costs through technological change, is that prices should be related to costs. Furthermore, if and when competition is preserved, price reductions follow cost reductions speedily and quite completely, for one of the major functions of competition is to relate price to cost. But if restrictions on competition are allowed to develop and expand, prices will not fall, for the major function of monopoly is to break the connection between cost and price and charge "all the traffic will bear." These divergent results are achieved because under competition demand and supply are kept in balance by fluctuations in price with volume of production well sustained, whereas monopoly attempts to achieve equilibrium by fixing the price and adjusting supply to demand through control and restriction of output. One leads to capacity production, full employment, and a high standard of living for all; the other leads to scarcity of goods, unemployment, high prices, and the enrichment of the few at the expense of the many. That is why Mills has told us that "From a social point of view it is desirable that gains in productivity should bring a larger output, with advanced living standards for consumers at large, rather than special advantage for some, coexisting with idleness of important productive resources. These ends may be most readily attained through a reduction in the selling prices of the finished goods immediately affected by the productivity gain, a reduction equivalent to the saving in cost of production."

By way of final comment the writer readily concedes that effective competition cannot be, and should not be, preserved in all industries and for all commodities. There are social monopolies arising from peculiar properties inherent in the business. Any attempt to set the price of public utility services in cities, or railroad rates, by the competitive technique would be absurd. Our contention is that, if and when we do find monopolistic areas where competition is no longer effective in fixing the price and the power to administer prices independent of costs has been achieved, the welfare of the nation and the future stability of business require that one of two things happen. Either monopolistic power should be destroyed and competition reestablished, which is the best solution wherever possible, or governmental commissions should be created with adequate legal power and a competent staff of price economists and cost accountants to see that reductions in cost are followed by reductions in price in order that the gains from technological progress shall not become the profits of the few. The suggestion by Means that the flexible prices of goods competitively produced can be brought to a parity with the administered prices of goods monopolistically produced by monetary management reveals a fundamental misconception of the basic problem involved.

II. THE DEPRESSION AS THE END OF AMERICAN ECONOMIC GROWTH

Iron Age: PROBLEMS OF INDUSTRIAL MATURITY

The following March 1931 editorial from Iron Age, *a prominent trade journal of the iron and steel industry, illustrates well the conclusion that many businessmen by that date were drawing from their experiences during the depression. Many of them were coming to the position that the era of rapid economic expansion in America had ended and that a closely coordinated, noncompetitive industrial system had become necessary.*

THE PERSPECTIVE of history may reveal the present depression as marking the transition from the development stage of our economic growth to the less spectacular and more settled ways of industrial maturity. Certain it is that the seemingly boundless markets that have stimulated the resourcefulness and energy of our people since they first set foot on this broad continent have finally been disclosed as having definite limits. Mass production, after acquiring great momentum under the spur of ever decreasing costs and constantly expanding sales, has run into the stone wall of saturated demand. The savings accruing from rapid growth are now a thing of the past in many industries, and future profits depend on replacement business and the slow increment that comes from increases in population.

It is true that saturation is a relative term and that true saturation will not arrive until the many millions of people still on a low economic scale are able to translate their wants into purchases. But it has become apparent that this potential buying power cannot be tapped by the simple formula of pushing more and more goods on the market. Nor is there any lasting benefit from artificially expanding demand through installment credit, an expedient that merely concentrates business in one period at the expense of the next.

Further broadening of effective demands can come only from genuine gains in general buying power. That desideratum will not be achieved by legislative meddling or by the grandiose schemes of theorists. Taking from Peter to give to Paul will not bring about a permanent readjustment. Business is not static; it is a dynamic, living thing and cannot safely be sapped to feed parasites. But its growth can be stimulated so that its fruits will be more abundant.

And greater fructification is a problem that managerial acumen is best equipped to solve. It implies further elimination of wastes. It implies a prevention of the prodigious losses arising from blind expansion of plant during cyclical upturns. It implies avoiding the cruel destruction of both material and human values resulting from unrestrained competition and the more general adoption of a "live and let live" policy. It implies foregoing

"Problems of Industrial Maturity," *Iron Age*, CXXVII, 11 (March 12, 1931), p. 880. Reprinted by permission of *Iron Age*.

immediate gain for the more permanent profits flowing from a sound and stable industrial order.

And extending our appraisal of future needs in terms of present indications, it seems clear that both capacity and production will be kept in closer step with actual demand; yet demand will not be stifled by exorbitant prices. Similarly, forbearance of competitor in relation to competitor and of seller in relation to the buyer will become the order of the day, while the partnership of employer and employee will become more closely knit. The "get rich quick" itch will give place to business statesmanship, which will seek the long-term returns that are possible only with the healthy growth of all parts of our economic organism. Wholehearted cooperation in grappling with the manifold problems of increasing interdependence will become as characteristic of our period of industrial maturity as narrow individualism was typical of the era of initial growth.

Franklin D. Roosevelt: IS THE ECONOMY OVERBUILT?

Earlier in the present volume one of President Roosevelt's 1938 speeches was used to illustrate a version of the underconsumption-overproduction interpretation of the depression. That Roosevelt also was aware of the "maturity thesis," however, is evident in these remarks taken from speeches of 1932–33. The following excerpts from the Commonwealth Club campaign address of September 1932 and from the second Fireside Chat of May 1933 indicate the wide acceptance which the businessman's view, exemplified by the preceding article from Iron Age, enjoyed during the campaign of 1932 and the early part of the Roosevelt presidency. These selections suggest, too, the role that this view played in the formation of policy at the beginning of the New Deal.

IN RETROSPECT we can now see that the turn of the tide came with the turn of the century. We were reaching our last frontier; there was no more free land and our industrial combinations had become great uncontrolled and irresponsible units of power within the State. Clear-sighted men saw with fear the danger that opportunity would no longer be equal; that the growing corporation, like the feudal baron of old, might threaten the economic freedom of individuals to earn a living. In that hour, our antitrust laws were born. The cry was raised against the great corporations. Theodore Roosevelt, the first great Republican Progressive, fought a Presidential campaign on the issue of "trust busting" and talked freely about malefactors of great wealth. If the Government had a policy it was rather to turn the clock back, to destroy the large combinations and to return to the time when every man owned his individual small business.

From the text in Samuel I. Rosenmann (comp.), *The Public Papers and Addresses of Franklin D. Roosevelt* (New York: Random House, 1938), I, pp. 749–53. The excerpt from the second Fireside Chat is taken from *ibid.*, II, pp. 163–65.

This was impossible; Theodore Roosevelt, abandoning the idea of "trust busting," was forced to work out a difference between "good" trusts and "bad" trusts. The Supreme Court set forth the famous "rule of reason" by which it seems to have meant that a concentration of industrial power was permissible if the method by which it got its power, and the use it made of that power, were reasonable.

Woodrow Wilson, elected in 1912, saw the situation more clearly. Where Jefferson had feared the encroachment of political power on the lives of individuals, Wilson knew that the new power was financial. He saw, in the highly centralized economic system, the despot of the twentieth century, on whom great masses of individuals relied for their safety and their livelihood, and whose irresponsibility and greed (if they were not controlled) would reduce them to starvation and penury. The concentration of financial power had not proceeded so far in 1912 as it has today, but it had grown far enough for Mr. Wilson to realize fully its implications. It is interesting, now, to read his speeches. What is called "radical" today (and I have reason to know whereof I speak) is mild compared to the campaign of Mr. Wilson. "No man can deny," he said, "that the lines of endeavor have more and more narrowed and stiffened; no man who knows anything about the development of industry in this country can have failed to observe that the larger kinds of credit are more and more difficult to obtain unless you obtain them upon terms of uniting your efforts with those who already control the industry of the country, and nobody can fail to observe that every man who tries to set himself up in competition with any process of manufacture which has taken place under the control of large combinations of capital will presently find himself either squeezed out or obliged to sell and allow himself to be absorbed." Had there been no World War — had Mr. Wilson been able to devote eight years to domestic instead of to international affairs — we might have had a wholly different situation at the present time. However, the then distant roar of European cannon, growing ever louder, forced him to abandon the study of this issue. The problem he saw so clearly is left with us as a legacy; and no one of us on either side of the political controversy can deny that it is a matter of grave concern to the Government.

A glance at the situation today only too clearly indicates that equality of opportunity as we have known it no longer exists. Our industrial plant is built; the problem just now is whether under existing conditions it is not overbuilt. Our last frontier has long since been reached, and there is practically no more free land. More than half of our people do not live on the farms or on lands and cannot derive a living by cultivating their own property. There is no safety valve in the form of a Western prairie to which those thrown out of work by the Eastern economic machines can go for a new start. We are not able to invite the immigration from Europe to share our endless plenty. We are now providing a drab living for our own people.

Our system of constantly rising tariffs has at last reacted against us to the point of closing our Canadian frontier on the north, our European markets on the east, many of our Latin-American markets to the south, and a goodly proportion of our Pacific markets on the west, through the retaliatory tariffs of those countries. It has forced many of our great industrial institutions which exported their surplus production to such countries, to establish plants in such countries, within the tariff walls. This has resulted in the reduction of the operation of their American plants, and opportunity for employment.

Just as freedom to farm has ceased, so also the opportunity in business has narrowed. It still is true that men can start small enterprises, trusting to native shrewdness and ability to keep abreast of competitors; but area after area has been preempted altogether by the great corporations, and even in the fields which still have no great concerns, the small man starts under a handicap. The unfeeling statistics of the past three decades show that the independent business man is running a losing race. Perhaps he is forced to the wall; perhaps he cannot command credit; perhaps he is "squeezed out," in Mr. Wilson's words, by highly organized corporate competitors, as your corner grocery man can tell you. Recently a careful study was made of the concentration of business in the United States. It showed that our economic life was dominated by some six hundred odd corporations who controlled two-thirds of American industry. Ten million small business men divided the other third. More striking still, it appeared that if the process of concentration goes on at the same rate, at the end of another century we shall have all American industry controlled by a dozen corporations, and run by perhaps a hundred men. Put plainly, we are steering a steady course toward economic oligarchy, if we are not there already.

Clearly, all this calls for a re-appraisal of values. A mere builder of more industrial plants, a creator of more railroad systems, an organizer of more corporations, is as likely to be a danger as a help. The day of the great promoter or the financial Titan, to whom we granted any-

thing if only he would build, or develop, is over. Our task now is not discovery or exploitation of natural resources, or necessarily producing more goods. It is the soberer, less dramatic business of administering resources and plants already in hand, of seeking to reestablish foreign markets for our surplus production, of meeting the problem of underconsumption, of adjusting production to consumption, of distributing wealth and products more equitably, of adapting existing economic organizations to the service of the people. The day of enlightened administration has come.

Just as in older times the central Government was first a haven of refuge, and then a threat, so now in a closer economic system the central and ambitious financial unit is no longer a servant of national desire, but a danger. I would draw the parallel one step farther. We did not think because national Government had become a threat in the 18th century that therefore we should abandon the principle of national Government. Nor today should we abandon the principle of strong economic units called corporations, merely because their power is susceptible of easy abuse. In other times we dealt with the problem of an unduly ambitious central Government by modifying it gradually into a constitutional democratic Government. So today we are modifying and controlling our economic units.

As I see it, the task of Government in its relation to business is to assist the development of an economic declaration of rights, an economic constitutional order. This is the common task of statesman and business man. It is the minimum requirement of a more permanently safe order of things.

Happily, the times indicate that to create such an order not only is the proper policy of Government, but it is the only line of safety for our economic structures as well. We know, now, that these economic units cannot exist unless prosperity is uniform, that is, unless purchasing power is well distributed throughout every group in the Nation. That is why even the most selfish of corporations for its own interest would be glad to see wages restored and unemployment ended and to bring the Western farmer back to his accustomed level of prosperity and to assure a permanent safety to both groups. That is why some enlightened industries themselves endeavor to limit the freedom of action of each man and business group within the industry in the common interest of all; why business men everywhere are asking a form of organization which will bring the scheme of things into balance, even though it may in some measure qualify the freedom of action of individual units within the business.

The exposition need not further be elaborated. It is brief and incomplete, but you will be able to expand it in terms of your own business or occupation without difficulty. I think everyone who has actually entered the economic struggle — which means everyone who was not born to safe wealth — knows in his own experience and his own life that we have now to apply the earlier concepts of American Government to the conditions of today.

The Declaration of Independence discusses the problem of Government in terms of a contract. Government is a relation of give and take, a contract, perforce, if we would follow the thinking out of which it grew. Under such a contract rulers were accorded power, and the people consented to that power on consideration that they be accorded certain rights. The task of statesmanship has always been the re-definition of these rights in terms of a changing and growing social order. New conditions impose new requirements upon Government and those who conduct Government.

*   *   *

Further legislation has been taken up which goes much more fundamentally into our economic problems. The Farm Relief Bill seeks by the use of several methods, alone or together, to bring about an increased return to farmers for their major farm products, seeking at the same time to prevent in the days to come disastrous overproduction which so often in the past has kept farm commodity prices far below a reasonable return. This measure provides wide powers for emergencies. The extent of its use will depend entirely upon what the future has in store.

Well-considered and conservative measures will likewise be proposed which will attempt to give to the industrial workers of the country a more fair wage return, prevent cut-throat competition and unduly long hours for labor, and at the same time encourage each industry to prevent overproduction.

Our Railroad Bill falls into the same class because it seeks to provide and make certain definite planning by the railroads themselves, with the assistance of the Government, to eliminate the duplication and waste that is now resulting in railroad receiverships and continuing operating deficits.

I am certain that the people of this country understand and approve the broad purposes behind these new governmental policies relating to agriculture and industry and transportation. We found ourselves faced with more agricultural products than we could possibly consume ourselves and with surpluses which other Nations did not have the cash to buy from us except at prices ruinously low. We found our factories able to turn out more goods than we could possibly consume, and at the same time we were faced with a falling export demand. We found ourselves with more facilities to transport goods and crops than there were goods and crops to be transported. All of this has been caused in large part by a complete lack of planning and a complete failure to understand the danger signals that have been flying ever since the close of the World War. The people of this country have been erroneously encouraged to believe that they could keep on increasing the output of farm and factory indefinitely and that some magician would find ways and means for that increased output to be consumed with reasonable profit to the producer.

Today we have reason to believe that things are a little better than they were two months ago. Industry has picked up, railroads are carrying more freight, farm prices are better, but I am not going to indulge in issuing proclamations of over-enthusiastic assurance. We cannot bally-hoo ourselves back to prosperity. I am going to be honest at all times with the people of the country. I do not want the people of this country to take the foolish course of letting this improvement come back on another speculative wave. I do not want the people to believe that because of unjustified optimism we can resume the ruinous practice of increasing our crop output and our factory output in the hope that a kind Providence will find buyers at high prices. Such a course may bring us immediate and false prosperity but it will be the kind of pros-

perity that will lead us into another tailspin.

It is wholly wrong to call the measures that we have taken Government control of farming, industry, and transportation. It is rather a partnership between Government and farming and industry and transportation, not partnership in profits, for the profits still go to the citizens, but rather a partnership in planning, and a partnership to see that the plans are carried out.

Let me illustrate with an example. Take the cotton-goods industry. It is probably true that 90 percent of the cotton manufacturers would agree to eliminate starvation wages, would agree to stop long hours of employment, would agree to stop child labor, would agree to prevent an overproduction that would result in unsalable surpluses. But, what good is such an agreement if the other 10 percent of cotton manufacturers pay starvation wages, require long hours, employ children in their mills and turn out burdensome surpluses? The unfair 10 percent could produce goods so cheaply that the fair 90 percent would be compelled to meet the unfair conditions. Here is where Government comes in. Government ought to have the right and will have the right, after surveying and planning for an industry, to prevent, with the assistance of the overwhelming majority of that industry, unfair practices and to enforce this agreement by the authority of Government. The so-called anti-trust laws were intended to prevent the creation of monopolies and to forbid unreasonable profits to those monopolies. That purpose of the antitrust laws must be continued, but these laws were never intended to encourage the kind of unfair competition that results in long hours, starvation wages and overproduction.

Alvin H. Hansen: SECULAR STAGNATION

Alvin H. Hansen, from his academic posts at the University of Minne-
sota and, beginning in 1937, at Harvard, has enjoyed one of the most
distinguished and influential careers witnessed by his profession. The
following selection is taken from his presidential address before the
American Economic Association in 1938.

EVERY period is in some sense a period of transition. The swift stream
of events in the last quarter century
offers, however, overwhelming testimony
in support of the thesis that the economic order of the western world is undergoing in this generation a structural
change no less basic and profound in
character than that transformation of
economic life and institutions which we
are wont to designate loosely by the
phrase "the Industrial Revolution." We
are passing, so to speak, over a divide
which separates the great era of growth
and expansion of the nineteenth century
from an era which no man, unwilling to
embark on pure conjecture, can as yet
characterize with clarity or precision. We
are moving swiftly out of the order in
which those of our generation were
brought up, into no one knows what.

Overwhelmingly significant, but as yet
all too little considered by economists, is
the profound change which we are currently undergoing in the rate of population growth. In the decade of the nine-
teen-twenties the population of the
United States increased by 16,000,000 —
an absolute growth equal to that of the
pre-war decade and in excess of any
other decade in our history. In the current decade we are adding only half this
number to our population, and the best
forecasts indicate a decline to a third in
the decade which we are about to enter.

Inadequate as the data are, it appears
that the prodigious growth of population
in the nineteenth century was something
unique in history. Gathering momentum
with the progress of modern science and
transportation, the absolute growth in
western Europe mounted decade by
decade until the great World War; and
in the United States it reached the highest level, as I have just noted, in the
post-war decade. The upward surge began with relatively small accretions
which rapidly swelled into a flood. But
the advancing tide has come to a sudden
halt and the accretions are dwindling
toward zero.

Thus, with the prospect of actual contraction confronting us, already we are
in the midst of a drastic decline in the
rate of population growth. Whatever the
future decades may bring, this present
fact is already upon us; and it behooves
us as economists to take cognizance of
the significance of this revolutionary
change in our economic life.

Schooled in the traditions of the Mal-
thusian theory, economists, thinking in
terms of static economies, have typically
placed an optimistic interpretation upon
the cessation of population growth. This
indeed is also the interpretation suggested by the National Resources Committee which recently has issued an ex-
haustive statistical inquiry into current
and prospective changes in population

From Alvin H. Hansen, "Economic Progress and Declining Population Growth," *American Economic
Review*, XXIX, 1 (March 1939), pp. 1–5, 7–8, 9–13. Reprinted by permission of the *American Economic Review* and of the author.

growth. In a fundamental sense this conclusion is, I think, thoroughly sound; for
it can scarcely be questioned that a continued growth of population at the rate
experienced in the nineteenth century
would rapidly present insoluble problems. But it would be an unwarranted
optimism to deny that there are implicit
in the current drastic shift from rapid
expansion to cessation of population
growth, serious structural maladjustments which can be avoided or mitigated
only if economic policies, appropriate to
the changed situation, are applied. Indeed in this shift must be sought a basic
cause of not a few of the developments
in our changing economy.

Adam Smith regarded growth of population as at once a consequence and a
cause of economic progress. Increasing
division of labor would, he argued, bring
about greater productivity, and this
would furnish an enlarged revenue and
stock, from which would flow an enlarged wages fund, an increased demand
for labor, higher wages, and so economic
conditions favorable for population
growth. Now a growing population, by
widening the market and by fostering
inventiveness, in turn facilitated, he
thought, division of labor and so the production of wealth. Thus he arrived at an
optimistic conclusion. Population growth,
he held, stimulated progress and this in
turn stimulated further growth and expansion. In contrast, the pessimistic analyses of Malthus and Richardo stressed
the limitation of natural resources and
the danger of an increasing population's
pressing down the margin of cultivation
to a point at which real income would
be reduced to a bare subsistence level.
In this static analysis the more dynamic
approach of Adam Smith was quite forgotten. If we wish to get a clear insight
into the economic consequences of the
current decline in population growth, it
is necessary to return to the suggestion
of Adam Smith and to explore more fully
the causal interconnection between economic progress, capital formation and
population growth.

Economic analysis from the earliest
development of our science has been
concerned with the rôle played by economic progress. Various writers have
included under this caption different
things; but for our purpose we may say
that the constituent elements of economic
progress are (a) inventions, (b) the discovery and development of new territory
and new resouces, and (c) the growth of
population. Each of these in turn, sever-
ally and in combination, has opened investment outlets and caused a rapid
growth of capital formation.

The earlier economists were concerned
chiefly with the effect of economic progress upon the volume of output, or in
other words, upon the level of real income. For them economic progress
affected the economic life mainly, if not
exclusively, in terms of rising productivity and higher real income per capita.

Not until the very end of the nineteenth century did an extensive literature
arise which stressed the rôle of economic
progress as a leading, if not the main,
factor causing fluctuations in employment, output, and income. Ricardo had
indeed seen that there was some relation
between economic progress and economic instability; but it was left for
Wicksell, Spiethoff, Schumpeter, Cassel,
and Robertson to elaborate the thesis
that economic fluctuations are essentially
a function of economic progress.

More recently the rôle of economic
progress in the maintenance of full employment of the productive resources has
come under consideration. The earlier
economists assumed that the economic

system tended automatically to produce full employment of resources. Some unemployment there was periodically, owing to the fluctuations incident to the business cycle; but in the upswing phase of the cyclical movement the economy was believed to function in a manner tending to bring about full recovery — maximum output and employment. This view was inspired by a century in which the forces of economic progress were powerful and strong, in which investment outlets were numerous and alluring. Spiethoff saw clearly that technological progress, the developmentof new industries, the discovery of new resources, the opening of new territory were the basic causes of the boom, which in turn was the progenitor of depression. Indeed he believed that once the main resources of the globe had been discovered and exploited, once the whole world had been brought under the sway of the machine technique, the leading disturbing factors which underlie the fluctuations of the cycle would have spent their force and an era of relative economic stability would ensue. But he did not raise the question whether such stability would be achieved at a full-employment and full-income level.

The business cycle was *par excellence* the problem of the nineteenth century. But the main problem of our times, and particularly in the United States, is the problem of full employment. Yet paradoxical as it may seem, the nineteenth century was little concerned with, and understood but dimly, the character of the business cycle. Indeed, so long as the problem of full employment was not pressing, it was not necessary to worry unduly about the temporary unemployment incident to the swings of the cycle. Not until the problem of full employment of our productive resources from the long-run, secular standpoint was

upon us, were we compelled to give serious consideration to those factors and forces in our economy which tend to make business recoveries weak and anemic and which tend to prolong and deepen the course of depressions. This is the essence of secular stagnation — sick recoveries which die in their infancy and depressions which feed on themselves and leave a hard and seemingly immovable core of unemployment.

In every great crisis the struggle of contending groups maneuvering for an advantageous position amidst rapid change whips up the froth and fury of political and social controversy. Always there is present the temptation to explain the course of events in terms of the more superficial phenomena which are frequently manifestations rather than causes of change. It is the peculiar function of the economist however to look deeper into the underlying economic realities and to discover in these, if possible, the causes of the most obstinate problem of our time — the problem of under-employment. Fundamental to an understanding of this problem are the changes in the "external" forces, if I may so describe them, which underlie economic progress — changes in the character of technological innovations, in the availability of new territory, and in the growth of population.

The expanding economy of the last century called forth a prodigious growth of capital formation. So much was this the case, that this era in history has by common consent been called the capitalistic period. No one disputes the thesis that without this vast accumulation of capital we should never have witnessed the great rise in the standard of living achieved since the beginning of the Industrial Revolution. But it is not the effect of capital formation upon real income to which I wish especially to direct attention. What I wish to stress in this paper is rather the rôle played by the process of capital formation in securing at each point in this ascending income scale fairly full employment of the productive resources and therefore the maximum income possible under the then prevailing level of technological development. For it is an indisputable fact that the prevailing economic system has never been able to reach reasonably full employment or the attainment of its currently realizable real income without making large investment expenditures. The basis for this imperious economic necessity has been thoroughly explored in the last half century in the great literature beginning with Tougan-Baranowsky and Wicksell on saving and investment. I shall not attempt any summary statement of this analysis. Nor is this necessary; for I take it that it is accepted by all schools of current economic thought that full employment and the maximum currently attainable income level cannot be reached in the modern free enterprise economy without a volume of investment expenditures adequate to fill the gap between consumption expenditures and that level of income which could be achieved were all the factors employed. In this somewhat truistic statement I hope I have succeeded in escaping a hornets' nest of economic controversy.

* * *

An interesting problem for statistical research would be to determine the proportion of investment in the nineteenth century which could be attributed (a) to population growth, (b) to the opening up of new territory and the discovery of new resources, and (c) to technical innovations. Such an analysis it has not been possible for me to make, and I shall venture only a few rough estimates to-

gether with some qualitative judgments. With respect to population growth some insight into the problem may perhaps be gained by considering first the rôle of population growth in the rise of aggregate real income. The various estimates agree that the annual rate of growth of physical output up to the World War was roughly three per cent in western Europe and nearly four per cent in the United States. Of this average annual increase something less than half of the three per cent increase in western Europe can be attributed to population growth, while something more than half of the annual increase in the United States can be assigned to the increase in the labor supply. Thus it appears that per capita output has increased both in western Europe and in the United States at approximately one and one-half per cent per annum. This increase can be attributed mainly to changes in technique and to the exploitation of new natural resources.

We have already noted that capital formation has progressed at about the same rate as the rise in aggregate output. Thus, as a first approximation, we may say that the growth of population in the last half of the nineteenth century was responsible for about forty per cent of the total volume of capital formation in western Europe and about sixty per cent of the capital formation in the United States. If this is even approximately correct, it will be seen what an important outlet for investment is being closed by reason of the current rapid decline in population growth.

* * *

It is not possible, I think, to make even an approximate estimate of the proportion of the new capital created in the nineteenth century which was a direct consequence of the opening up of new territory. The development of new countries was indeed so closely intertwined with the growth of population that it would be difficult to avoid double counting. What proportion of new capital formation in the United States went each year into the western frontier we do not know, but it must have been very considerable. Apparently about one-fourth of the total capital accumulation of England was invested abroad by 1914, and one-seventh of that of France.

These figures, while only suggestive, point unmistakably to the conclusion that the opening of new territory and the growth of population were together responsible for a very large fraction — possibly somewhere near one-half — of the total volume of new capital formation in the nineteenth century. These outlets for new investment are rapidly being closed. The report on *Limits of Land Settlement* by President Isaiah Bowman and others may be regarded as conclusive in its findings that there are no important areas left for exploitation and settlement. So far as population is concerned, that of western Europe has already virtually reached a standstill; but that in eastern Europe, notably in Russia, is still growing, and so also is that in the Orient. And much of this area will probably experience a considerable industrialization. But it is not yet clear how far the mature industrial countries will participate in this development through capital export. Russia still has a long way to go before she becomes completely industrialized; but foreign capital is not likely to play any significant rôle in this process. India will offer some opportunity for British investment, but the total is likely to be small relative to the volume of British foreign investments in the nineteenth century. China and the Orient generally offer, in view of the present

and prospective turmoil in that area, relatively meager investment opportunities. At all events, no one is likely to challenge the statement that foreign investment will in the next fifty years play an incomparably smaller rôle than was the case in the nineteenth century.

Thus the outlets for new investment are rapidly narrowing down to those created by the progress of technology. To be sure, the progress of technology itself played in the nineteenth century a decisive rôle in the opening of new territory and as a stimulus to population growth. But while technology can facilitate the opening of new territory, it cannot create a new world or make the old one bigger than it is. And while the advance of science, by reducing the death rate, was a major cause of the vast nineteenth-century increase in population, no important further gains in this direction can possibly offset the prevailing low birth rate. Thus the further progress of science can operate to open investment outlets only through its direct influence on the technique of production.

We are thus rapidly entering a world in which we must fall back upon a more rapid advance of technology than in the past if we are to find private investment opportunities adequate to maintain full employment. Should we accept the advice of those who would declare a moratorium on invention and technical progress, this one remaining avenue for private investment would also be closed. There can be no greater error in the analysis of the economic trends of our times than that which finds in the advance of technology, broadly conceived, a major cause of unemployment. It is true that we cannot discount the problem of technological unemployment, a problem which may be intensified by the apparently growing importance of capital-saving inventions. But, on the other side, we cannot afford to neglect the type of innovation which creates new industries and which thereby opens new outlets for real investment. The problem of our generation is, above all, the problem of inadequate private investment outlets. What we need is not a slowing down in the progress of science and technology, but rather an acceleration of that rate.

Of first-rate importance is the development of new industries. There is certainly no basis for the assumption that these are a thing of the past. But there is equally no basis for the assumption that we can take for granted the rapid emergence of new industries as rich in investment opportunities as the railroad, or more recently the automobile, together with all the related developments, including the construction of public roads, to which it gave rise. Nor is there any basis, either in history or in theory, for the assumption that the rise of new industries proceeds inevitably at a uniform pace. The growth of modern industry has not come in terms of millions of small increments of change giving rise to a smooth and even development. Characteristically it has come by gigantic leaps and bounds. Very often the change can best be described as discontinuous, lumpy, and jerky, as indeed D. H. Robertson has so vividly done. And when a revolutionary new industry like the railroad or the automobile, after having initiated in its youth a powerful upward surge of investment activity, reaches maturity and ceases to grow, as all industries finally must, the whole economy must experience a profound stagnation, unless indeed new developments take its place. It is not enough that a mature industry continues its activity at a high level on a horizontal plane. The fact that

new railroad mileage continued to be built at about the same rate through the seventies, eighties and nineties was not sufficient. It is the *cessation of growth* which is disastrous. It is in connection with the growth, maturity and decline of great industries that the principle of acceleration operates with peculiar force. And when giant new industries have spent their force, it *may* take a long time before something else of equal magnitude emerges. In fact nothing has emerged in the decade in which we are now living. This basic fact, together with the virtual cessation of public investment by state and local governmental bodies, as indicated by a decline of $2,000,000,000 in their net public debt since 1932, explains in large measure the necessary rise in federal expenditures.

❖   ❖   ❖

We have noted that the approaching cessation of population growth and the disappearance of new territory for settlement and exploitation may cut off a half or more of the investment outlets which we were wont to make in the past. We are thus compelled to fall back upon that measure of capital formation which is associated with the advance of technique and the rise in per capita output. But current institutional developments are restricting even this outlet. The growing power of trade unions and trade associations, the development of monopolistic competition, of rivalry for the market through expensive persuasion and advertising, instead of through price competition, are factors which have rightly of late commanded much attention among economists. There is, moreover, the tendency to block the advance of technical progress by the shelving of patents.

Under vigorous price competition, new cost-reducing techniques were compulsorily introduced even though the scrapping of obsolete but undepreciated machinery entailed a capital loss. But under the monopoly principle of obsolescence new machines will not be introduced until the undepreciated value of the old machine will at least be covered by the economies of the new technique. Thus progress is slowed down, and outlets for new capital formation, available under a more ruthles competitove society, are cut off. Capital losses which could not be avoided under rigorous price competition can be and are avoided under an economic system more closely integrated by intercorporate association and imperfect competition. If we are to save the one remaining outlet for private capital formation, deliberate action of a far bolder character than hitherto envisaged must be undertaken in order to make the price system and free enterprise sufficiently responsive to permit at least that measure of capital formation to which the rate of technological progress had accustomed us in the past.

Yet even though this much were achieved, it is necessary to recognize that such a rate of progress would not provide sufficient investment outlets to give us full employment of our resources. With a stationary population we could maintain as rapid a rise in per capita real income as that experienced in the past, by making annually only half the volume of new investment to which we have been accustomed. A volume of investment adequate to provide full employment could give us an annual percentage increase in per capita output greatly in excess of any hitherto attained.

*   *   *

As so often in economic life, we are confronted by a dilemma. Continued unemployment on a vast scale, resulting from inadequate private investment outlets, could be expected sooner or later to lead straight into an all-round regimented economy. But so also, by an indirect route and a slower process, might a greatly extended program of public expenditures. And from the standpoint of economic workability the question needs to be raised how far such a program can be carried out in a democratic society without raising the cost structure to a level which prevents full employment. Thus a challenge is presented to all those countries which have not as yet submitted to the yoke of political dictatorship. In one of our round tables we are discussing divergencies in the success of governmental spending in democratic countries and in totalitarian states. Totalitarian states have the great advantage that they can rigorously check the advance of costs, including wage rates, while engaging in an expansionist program of public investment. Democratic countries cannot in modern times escape from the influence exerted by organized groups upon the operation of the price system. From the standpoint of the workability of the system of free enterprise, there emerges the problem of sovereignty in democratic countries confronted in their internal economies with powerful groups — entrepreneurial and wage-earning — which have robbed the price system of that impersonal and nonpolitical character idealized in the doctrine of laissez-faire. It remains still to be seen whether political democracy can in the end survive the disappearance of the automatic price system.

Glenn E. McLaughlin and Ralph J. Watkins: PITTSBURGH, A CASE STUDY OF SECULAR STAGNATION

Glenn E. McLaughlin and Ralph J. Watkins were members of the University of Pittsburgh Economics Department when they presented this study at the annual meeting of the American Economic Association in December 1938.

THE MAIN QUESTION

CAN THE [American] system produce a progressive evolution of the economy and the upbuilding of the standard of living of the American people? . . . The present paper is concerned with . . . industrial growth in a mature economy, that is to say, with secular tendencies.

MEANING OF MATURITY

We shall not attempt here a precise formulation of the meaning of industrial maturity, nor shall we undertake to explore the causes of maturity. In passing we do voice the surmise that such formulation and exploration would lead one into a profound discussion of societal forms, of the emergence and disintegration of organizational patterns and techniques, and perhaps of the rhythmic surges of the human spirit itself. It scarcely needs be said that neither this forum nor these authors would be appropriate for that type of discussion. It is in point, however, to sketch some of the earmarks of industrial maturity.

The first evidence of maturity probably lies in the decrease in the rate of growth of heavy industries and of building activity, especially of factory construction. Maturity also involves the slowing down of the rate of growth of the total quantity of production, of employment, and usually of population. It probably will involve the rising relative importance of consumers goods. Lessened demand for capital in producers goods industries — mining, heavy manufacturing, and probably construction — can be expected, and a decrease in the rate of interest unless there is an offsetting increase in the demand for consumers goods. Such an offsetting increase is not likely to occur if there is a slowing down in population growth. If the sources of capital are withheld because of the low rate of interest, because of painful memories of capital losses, because of a pessimism bred of inspection of mature trends, or because of fear of public interventions made necessary politically by those mature trends, then maturity may be quickly transformed into decay.

With this picture in our minds, let us examine the record of industrial growth of the American economy with particular reference to the dominant industries on which this industrial growth has depended.

HISTORICAL RECORD OF DEPENDENCE ON DOMINANT INDUSTRIES

Throughout the colonial period and until the middle of the nineteenth century, agriculture remained the business of at least two-thirds of the population and was in all likelihood the major outlet for investment. Capital and enterprise found

From Glenn E. McLaughlin and Ralph J. Watkins, "The Problem of Industrial Growth in a Mature Economy," *American Economic Review*, Vol. XXIX, 1 (Supplement) (March 1939). Reprinted by permission of the *American Economic Review* and of the authors.

their richest rewards in the settlement of the West, in land speculation, and in the production of staples for the Seaboard or the European market. But, during this period, shipping absorbed large amounts of capital and labor, and from the end of the War of 1812 to the depression of 1837 this country led in transatlantic commerce and in the building of vessels, for both domestic and foreign shippers. In some years the net earnings of shipping almost equaled the total value of agricultural exports. These two decades saw also heavy investment in turnpikes and canals, which along with other internal improvements resulted in a great importation of European capital.

In general, infant manufacturing ventures were not very successful in competition with shipping and agriculture for the meager sources of local capital. For the most part, manufacturers had to finance expansion out of slowly cumulating profits. To a considerable extent, textile production was an exception, aided as it was by the acquisition of surplus funds from the whaling industry. On the other hand, the growth of the more typical iron industry was financed mainly from the comparatively high rate of return it earned as a result of the growing use of tools and machinery, both in agriculture and in manufacturing.

After 1840, the rise of the railroads absorbed large amounts of capital and stimulated the development of manufacturing and farming in the interior of the country. As extensive industrialization got under way, the production process became more "round about." Heavier investments were required because of the use of more complicated machinery and the introduction of a more detailed division of labor. Capital funds in manufacturing were estimated in census returns to have increased from 50 million dollars

in 1820 to 250 millions in 1840 and to 1 billion in 1860. The outstanding branch of manufacturing in 1860 was the production of flour and meal, which alone accounted for one-fourth of the total value of manufactured products. The most notable fields for investment in the next forty years — i.e., up to the turn of the century — were the railroads, iron and steel, coal, meat packing, and machinery. In 1900, the value of iron and steel products exceeded 800 million dollars, and the output of coal had risen to 212 million tons in comparison with 6 million tons in 1860. From 1850 to 1900, the population of the country trebled, the production of agriculture almost trebled, and the value of manufactures increased elevenfold. The industrial giant was clearly striking his stride.

The twentieth century has witnessed not only an accelerated pace in industrialization but also the rise of important new outlets for capital. Prominent among these are the automobile industry, the electric equipment industry, the petroleum industry, the electric utility industry, and urban construction.

EVIDENCES OF MATURITY

Despite the phenomenal industrial gains in the American economy, there are increasing signs of retardation of both population and industrial growth, signs which suggest that the United States is approaching a stage of industrial maturity. The special committee on population problems of the National Resources Committee has estimated that maximum population will be attained within one or two generations, the most optimistic peak being set at 187 million people in 1980 and the most probable at 154 million in 1980. . . . Among nearly all major industries, there has been a notable slowing down in the rate of growth since the World War. In some industries, production trends are horizontal or negatively inclined. Coal production has tended to drop since the World War, and there has been a significant downward trend in railroad passenger traffic since 1920, the present traffic volume being only about one-half what it was at that time. Although production trends continue moderately upward in steel, some branches of the industry, notably rails and wire rods, are characterized by falling trends. Passenger automobile production was roughly 15 per cent lower in 1937 than in 1929, although the trend of the industry may still be upward. Railroad freight traffic has also failed to pass its 1929 peak. Moreover, it is problematical whether the construction industry will soon pass its 1928 peak. Newer industries which have taken large amounts of capital in recent years also appear to be expanding at slower rates; examples are oil and gas and rubber. Indeed, retardation in growth appears to have taken place in the great majority of major American industries. Arthur F. Burns has shown that there is considerable evidence that most individual industries in agriculture, mining, and manufacture have experienced abatement in their rates of growth and that very likely this abatement is true as well of the individual branches of forestry, fisheries, construction, transportation, and trade.

Nor is there any great likelihood that the rates of industrial growth for major industries will stop falling. Within the past two decades there has been continued retardation of growth in older industries, and new industries have not developed fast enough to maintain a constant rate of increase in the total volume of goods produced. In an old, complex economy many new industries are required from time to time if the trend of

industrial production is not to fall, but in such an economy new industries are increasingly difficult to develop. The revival of rapid growth in an old industry usually requires a revolutionary change in the industrial arts. Generally, only in the early stages of development is the introduction of improvements rapid. Technical progress, in other words, proceeds at a declining rate, because the possibilities of important changes are more and more difficult to uncover. In this connection, Mr. William S. Knudsen, president of General Motors Corporation, in his recent testimony before the Temporary National Economic Committee, stated that it was virtually impossible at this stage in the development of the automobile industry that anyone would come upon a revolutionary invention. Likewise, Mr. Charles F. Kettering, vice-president of the same corporation, stated, "I don't see how that revolutionary thing could happen, especially in a highly developed art like automobile manufacturing. You just can't flash one of those things out. We have made about 45,000,000 automobiles now and the engineers have scraped those bones pretty carefully." Although we have seen the development within recent decades of dramatic new industries, such as the airplane, radio, air conditioning, and chemical industries, their importance has not been sufficient to affect materially the aggregate trend lines of industrial output.

Within the nation are several older, more mature industrial areas. The experience of such an area may give some clues to the kinds of problems which arise in a mature economy: problems concerned with the creation of capital; with the outlet for savings; with the growing conservatism of investors; with the intensive use of capital and the mech-

anization of industry; with the application of capital to social needs; with the
changing internal structure of the economy; and with the under-utilization of
capital and labor. The Pittsburgh district
is a mature industrial area whose growth
trends began to taper off almost thirty
years ago; and these problems there are
acute ones. In the belief, therefore, that
the Pittsburgh district offers an instructive case study of the problem of industrial growth in a mature economy, we
shall turn our attention to a discussion
of the clinical records of that regional
economy.

THE PITTSBURGH DISTRICT AS AN EXAMPLE OF INDUSTRIAL MATURITY

Basic Nature of Pittsburgh Industries

Pittsburgh is dominated by iron and
steel, bituminous coal, electrical equipment, foundry and machine shop products (especially heavy machinery), and
glass. These products, however, enter so
widely into the making of consumers
goods that changes in their output reflect
general movements in industry. The
major forms of industrial activity in the
Pittsburgh district are all capital goods
industries, but these industries have fur-
nished the major basis for national industrial growth. The trends of Pittsburgh
industry, therefore, are closely tied to
the stage of development of industry in
the country as a whole. Whenever the
trends in manufacturing and construction in the country begin to flatten out, as
in recent years, there is a sharp reduction in the new requirements for capital
equipment and building materials. Thus,
producers goods industries are peculiarly
sensitive to broad industrial changes.
Hence, Pittsburgh's industrial changes
may in a measure indicate what may be
anticipated in the national economy.

*Comparison of Industrial Production
Trends, Pittsburgh District and the
United States*

The Pittsburgh industrial district had
its rapid growth before 1909; until that
time the annual rate of growth in industrial production in the district was greater
than that in the United States. In the
past thirty years, however, Pittsburgh
has been in a comparatively mature stage
of development and has been growing
less rapidly than the country as a whole.
Growth in industrial production in the
district began to taper off noticeably
after 1909, whereas national industrial
production did not show definite signs
of slowing down until after the World
War. Industrially speaking, the Pittsburgh district reached maturity about
two decades ahead of the country generally. Pittsburgh had its years of rapid
industrial growth in the seventies, eighties, and nineties of the nineteenth century and in the first decade of the twentieth century, whereas national industrial
growth has continued until recent years
to feel the stimulation of rapid industrialization of the newer centers in the
Midwest, in the South, in the Southwest,
and on the Pacfic Coast. Many of those
centers will doubtless continue to grow
rapidly, but areas of rapidly growing industrialization are becoming smaller as
proportions of the total national economy. At the present time the composite
industrial production trend line is advancing at about one-half per cent per
year in the Pittsburgh district and at almost one and one-half per cent in the
United States. . . . The Pittsburgh district, because of the basic nature of its
industries and because of its later stage
of industrial development, may serve as
a guide to later developments in the
national economy.

Economic Development of the Pittsburgh District

The first manufacturing industries in the Pittsburgh district were those supplying consumers goods for the local population and for settlers moving farther west. After a time this western community began to specialize more in the exploitation of local resources — in the making of iron, heavy machinery, glass, and pottery — and for the most part gave up supplying local consumers' needs for manufactured articles. Railroad operation reduced transportation costs and allowed the exchange of local specialties for eastern manufactures. Thus, during the latter half of the nineteenth century western Pennsylvania became firmly integrated into the national economy when the district began to exploit its geographical position for the production of iron. The iron industry first became integrated in Pittsburgh, where Connellsville coke was used with Lake Superior ore. Thus, the main geographic advantages of the city in the iron industry consisted in its location near supplies of coal and near enough to Lake Erie to obtain relatively low freight costs on necessary supplies of ore.

During the 1870's industrial production in the Pittsburgh area was growing at a rising rate. Both coal and steel were expanding rapidly. Large amounts of capital were brought in from Philadelphia and New York, and the Pittsburgh district, which had started to develop industrially much later than these seaboard regions, began to grow more rapidly. The maximum rate of increase in population and in industrial production in the Pittsburgh area appears to have come during the 1880's. Population was increasing 4 per cent per year, largely owing to immigration. This influx was brought about largely by the rapid expansion of the iron and steel industry and the related increases in coal production. Great Bessemer converters and extensive crucible steel plants were constructed during this and the preceding decades. The steel industry was growing at a fast pace, owing mainly to the substitution of steel for iron in the making of railroad rails and structural forms. The Pittsburgh area was clearly in the stage of rapid growth. During this decade the annual growth of industrial production in Pittsburgh district was 10 per cent, or double that in the United States. During the 1890's the development of the open-hearth process greatly improved the quality of steel and led to the acquisition of new markets and to the further expansion of output. These gains, however, were not sufficient to maintain the rates of population and industrial growth, although the gains in each remained high. After 1900, expansion of the local iron and steel industry began to slow up, and immigration into the area was retarded. By 1910 the era of rapid population and industrial growth was completed. In the decade ended in 1930 the annual rate of population increase fell to 1.4 per cent, and the trend in steel production became almost horizontal. Industrial production continued to grow at about one-half per cent per year.

Present Growth Patterns of Major Industries

Most of Pittsburgh's leading industries are comparatively old. The steel industry there is characterized by a rate of growth not far from zero, and coal and coke production show declining trends. The district is so dominated by these and related industries that comparatively favorable rates of growth in glass, electrical equipment, and aluminum are of only minor assistance in raising the trend of total industrial output. Even if new industries appear, they will for a long time be dwarfed by the overwhelming importance of the older forms of economic activity. The absence of any new major activity in the twentieth century is worthy of note in connection with the marked retardation about 1909 in industrial growth and indirectly in population growth. Although none of the new important industries which have developed in the United States in the past forty years have taken root in Pittsburgh, many of them have been large consumers of coal, steel, heavy machinery, and glass, in part obtained from western Pennsylvania. Aluminum, electrical equipment, and glass are three industries which have apparently not yet reached maturity in the Pittsburgh district and which have continued to exercise a stimulating influence on manufacturing activity — even though overshadowed by coal and steel. Other forms of manufacturing which are growing rapidly are included mainly in the category of consumers' industries. . . .

Structural Changes in the Pittsburgh District

The major post-War changes affecting the industrial structure of the Pittsburgh district have been the decrease in coal production; the marked slowing down of expansion in manufacturing output; exceedingly rapid increases in service activities; the continued shift of manufacturing operations from the nucleus city to the smaller industrial cities in the periphery, especially along the Ohio, Monongahela, and Allegheny rivers; the increasing centralization of the district's service functions in Allegheny County, and mainly in Pittsburgh; and in many counties the decreasing relative importance of employment in mining and manufacturing and, within manufacturing industries, the decreasing relative importance of the iron and steel industry. Some of these diverse tendencies within the Pittsburgh district had their counterparts within the nation and thus reflected a general shift in the national economy under which fewer workers were required in coal mining and manufacturing and more in the manifold and growing trade and other service functions which rising standards of living and increasing specialization demand. Other changes represent the rise of a metropolitan economy and the co-ordination of the various activities of the district on a regionalized basis. Thus, the increase in the number of persons engaged in service functions in Allegheny County reflects the growing extent to which the nucleus city and its environs take over trade and other service functions for a large metropolitan area and tributary economic region — functions concerned not merely with management control and financial direction but also with all the varied recreational, cultural, governmental, health, and social activities that go to make up the life of a region.

Effects of Slowing Down of Growth

Retardation of industrial growth in the Pittsburgh district has been accompanied by large exports of capital to other parts of the country, for investment both in industries familiar to Pittsburghers and in newer forms of productive activity and by more intensive development and expansion of local industrial concerns. On the other hand, industrial maturity seems to have brought with it greater likelihood of under-utilization of labor and capital, greater susceptibility to wide cyclical swings in production and employment, and shortage of capital for social improvements.

Pittsburgh became an important investment center at about the time that it began to show signs of industrial maturity. Indeed, somewhat earlier there were evidences that capital and men were moving from Pittsburgh mainly to the West, South, and Southwest to establish newer concerns in the steel, coal, and petroleum industries. With the arrival of full maturity after the World War, Pittsburgh's need for "economic colonies" became acute, and large quantities of local savings — and War profits — were invested in other districts, primarily in steel and oil but also in sulphur, aluminum, glass, electrical equipment, food canning, public utilities, and a great variety of other forms of business. In part, outside investments have taken the form of branch plants of Pittsburgh-controlled concerns or of fellow subsidiaries where the Pittsburgh operating concern was controlled elsewhere. For example, large amounts of Pittsburgh profits must have gone into the development of the Gary steel district. More recently, the development of Pittsburgh as an important investment banking center, containing as it does one of the country's major underwriting groups for the sale of new securities, has facilitated the flow of Pittsburgh savings through investment channels to all parts of the country as well as abroad.

Industrial maturity and the absence of important new industries have meant that if Pittsburgh capital was to be invested locally it had to be used primarily in the futher mechanization and rationalization of Pittsburgh's industries. This intensive investment is exemplified in the steel industry by the construction of continuous rolling mills, in the coal industry by mechanization of mining methods and transportation, and in the glass industry by the development of new manufacturing processes. Moreover, the turning back of capital into the same industry has required the careful study of investment opportunities and has led to the organization of large research laboratories in the district, particularly those in steel, coal, oil, glass, and aluminum. Some Pittsburgh capital no doubt is being used in the development of new local industries, but in such a mature area of a large proportion of capital funds must be exported.

In the peak year of 1929 there was considerable under-utilization of capital and labor. In most of the months of that year from 5 to 10 per cent of the workers were entirely without jobs. Moreover, those who had jobs suffered appreciable loss of working time in that year, being idle in various months from 4 to 16 per cent of the time. For the normally gainfully employed population as a whole, total unemployment and underemployment of those with jobs have been estimated for 1929 as the equivalent of total unemployment of all workers, 14 per cent of the time. Average overcapacity of plant facilities during that year was probably of the same general order of magnitude or greater. From 1929 to 1932 the declines in employment and production were drastic. For example, man-hours in manufacturing industries fell 59 per cent from the 1929 average; and the volume of industrial production declined 62 per cent. Total unemployment at the low point (August, 1932), according to published estimates, amounted to almost 40 per cent of the normally gainfully employed population.

Although the evidence is not entirely convincing, the fifty-five-year record of industrial production in the Pittsburgh district seems to indicate that cyclical swings have become more severe and that under-utilization has tended to last longer as the economy has become more mature. This relationship is probably not a chance one, because a sharp upward trend in industrial production is exceedingly effective in wiping out the effects of past errors in judgment and in canceling the losses of depression. Thus a given depression is not so tragic in its consequences if growth is so rapid that the preceding peak is destined to be exceeded in level by the trough of the next depression. This relationship obtained in the Pittsburgh district during the seventies, eighties, and nineties and into the nineteenth hundreds up to 1907. Thereafter, the story has been painfully different, so much so that the 1932 trough was lower than the trend value for 1901, and the low month of June, 1938, was only slightly above the 1901 average. Certainly, it can be said that the greater industrialization and urbanization that have come with increasing maturity have heightened the vulnerability of the district's population to cyclical swings. Moreover, the growing relative scale of monetary expenditures — another concomitant of maturity — has probably had the effect of increasing both intensity of cyclical fluctuations and vulnerability to depression.

Economic Outlook for the Pittsburgh District

In summary, the economic outlook for the Pittsburgh district is that of a mature economy. No great change appears likely in the present annual increment of about 0.5 per cent per year in the trend of industrial production, and the rate of population growth in the 1920's of 1.4 per cent per year is almost certain to be lowered. The necessary acceleration of industrial growth adequate to support an annual increase in population in the Pittsburgh district of 1.4 per cent per year does not appear imminent. Unless the area witnesses another great expansion of service occupations, the basis for which is not in sight continued migration to other districts appears probable.

Pittsburgh's industries are old and basic. They are dependent on such a great variety of consuming industries that only a general outburst of national productive activity is likely to lead to a material increase in their rates of growth. Moreover, since new industries of considerable size do not appear to be in prospect in the district in the immediate future, not more than a continuation of the slow-growth trends established during the past quarter of a century can be expected. Consequently, unless the rate of population growth drops or migration from the area continues, there is a strong probability of a slow decrease in per capita income.

In the Pittsburgh district, the demand for capital will probably be largely for the purpose of making replacements. Excess savings are likely in the main to be invested in other areas as in the past three decades. One of the major problems of industrial maturity is likely to be the shortage of capital for improving social conditions. Many social and governmental problems created during the boom stage of development have been left for solution in the stage of industrial maturity — when the cost can be least afforded. Moreover, the very effort to solve these problems is likely to aggravate their nature. When a region reaches industrial maturity, there is always the danger that industry may begin to move away from the area and from the problems which it has created, a movement that may likely be accelerated by efforts to solve those social problems created by prior growth. Further, those who have retained much of the profits of the period of rapid growth are likely to move along with their savings to other and greener pastures or at least to send their capital to more promising fields. Thus the social consciousness that develops with industrial maturity may develop too late for effective action. Its very development may, in fact, accelerate the process of decay; and what was a mature area may become a depressed and stranded area. Some of these problems with respect to the improvement of living conditions and with respect to the solution of governmental problems threaten to become acute ones in the Pittsburgh district. Adequate housing and civic, recreational, and health facilities were not provided when the area was producing wealth rapidly. It may be impossible to provide these services at a time when most of the capital funds of the area are invested elsewhere. "It may be later than we think," but if it is too late — within the framework of an enterprise system — then from the people of that area we can, in our judgment, expect increasing pressures in the direction of public and joint private and public investment.

CONCLUSIONS

Attention has been devoted in this paper to the Pittsburgh district as a case study in industrial maturity, in the conviction that Pittsburgh's experience with industrial maturity during the past three decades is instructive to the nation; that the sorts of social and economic problems encountered there are likely in some degree to be met with in the nation over the coming years. In order that we may bring into sharp relief what we consider the lessons of that experience, we shall now attempt to outline some of the problems of industrial maturity that we anticipate will require the attention of those in industry and government who must concern themselves with economic and social policy:

1. Slowing down of industrial trends means a diminished opportunity for investment and a discouragement to initiative.

2. Under these circumstances investors become increasingly cautious and conservative; investment is primarily for replacement and for the more intensive use of capital through mechanization and improvement of processes.

3. Both investors and enterprisers turn their attention to more promising fields elsewhere, thus seeking "economic colonies" for investment and development.

4. These tendencies further aggravate the problem of industrial growth since they tend to deprive the economy of both capital funds and aggressive enterprisers.

5. The slowing-down process of industrial maturity is likely to be especially devastating in its effects on real estate values, leading to stagnation or retrogression in these values and thereby cutting off the flow of investment into construction, with a consequent further depressing influence on industrial trends.

6. Industrial maturity is likely to bring with it more serious and more frequent periods of under-utilization of the factors of production.

7. Shortage of capital for social improvements develops just at the time when social consciousness emerges to demand such improvements. The political pressures supporting these demands are likely to lead to measures which further undermine that economy or weaken its position with respect to other economies which stand in a competitive relation to it, either as investment outlets or as market outlets.

In short, it is probably fair to say that an enterprise system functions best in an expanding economy; and that the appearance of industrial maturity raises profound questions concerning the ability of an enterprise system to produce a progressive evolution of the economy under conditions of maturity. We believe that it is essentially these questions which lie behind the transformation of economies throughout the world in recent years — transformations involving increasing public participation. The problem of the American economy is to adjust itself to these influences and at the same time to preserve the maximum benefits of an enterprise system. This problem is not a simple one; rather, it will require cooperation of a high order between industry and government — industrial statesmanship as well as political statesmanship.

Joseph A. Schumpeter: "SOCIAL ATMOSPHERE" AND THE FUTURE OF CAPITALISM: A PESSIMISTIC APPRAISAL

In 1932 Joseph A. Schumpeter came to this country permanently as a Harvard professor after a varied career in Austria and Germany as government official and teacher. His books, notably The Theory of Economic Development (1911), Business Cycles (1939), *and* Capitalism, Socialism, and Democracy (1942), *have influenced American economic and historical thought immeasurably by focusing attention upon the importance of the entrepreneur and his innovating function in economic and social development. The following excerpt appears in the final section of* Business Cycles.

AS APPLIED to the American situation of today, . . . the theory that the capitalist process is stagnating from internal causes inherent to its logic and that income generation by government is nothing but the self-defense of a shriveling organism, is . . . a complete misfit — at best a mistaken interpretations of certain aftereffects of the world depression, at worst the product of wishful thinking on the part of all those who crave a presentable basis for policies they approve. It still retains two merits, however. The one consists in the many elements of truth which, as we have seen, enter into its arguments as distinguished from its application. The other consists in the recognition, by implication at least, of the fact that, as any social system depends for its functioning and survival on

the actual delivery of the premia it holds out, so capitalism depends for its functioning and survival on the actual delivery of the returns, anticipation of which provides its motive power. For this, after all, is what the stressing of investment opportunity amounts to. Slightly extending and modifying the meaning of that phrase, we may hence continue to use it ourselves and *agree* that it is vanishing investment opportunity which is the matter with present-day capitalism — anything can, in fact, be put into that form, the structural principles of the capitalist process being what they are. And our task then reduces to substituting for unconvincing reasons why investment opportunity should be vanishing, a more convincing one.

The analysis [above] supplies it: capitalism produces by its mere working a social atmosphere — a moral code, if the reader prefer — that is hostile to it, and this atmosphere, in turn, produces policies which do not allow it to function. There is no equilibrating apparatus to guarantee that this atmosphere or these policies should develop in such a way as to prevail in the fullness of time, *i.e.*, when the capitalist process will have really spent its force or be spending it. Whenever they prevail sooner, there is danger of a deadlock, by which we mean a situation in which neither capitalism nor its possible alternatives are workable. This is what, to a certain extent and presumably not yet for good, has happened in this country.

It might be replied that anticapitalist attitudes are also, like the tendencies adduced by the theory of vanishing investment opportunity in its usual acceptance, a matter of slow growth and, hence, similarly open to one of the objections raised against that theory above. But we are able to do in this case what cannot be done for those tendencies, *viz.*, to show that, and how, that attitude came *suddenly* to a head and suddenly acquired dominating importance. And anticapitalist policies, unlike attitudes, may be dated. The coincidence in time between them and disappointing performance of the economic engine is indeed striking. We will survey them under the headings of Fiscal, Labor, and — for want of a better expression — Industrial policies.

At least since 1932 the burden of direct taxation imposed upon that part of the national revenue which goes to the higher and highest brackets was undoubtedly high enough to affect "subjective" investment opportunity or, as we have previously expressed it, to shift the watershed between "to do and not to do." No other than direct or mechanical effects

need, however, be attributed to this burden until roughly 1933–1934, because the increase in taxation was then accepted as a sacrifice to be made in a national emergency, as it had been during the war. But from the revenue act of 1934 on, this was no longer so. Permanence of the burden for reasons unconnected with emergency, involving a transfer or redistribution of wealth which in the highest brackets amounted to the socialization of the bulk of private income, and in some cases taxation for taxation's sake and regardless of insignificance of results for the Treasury, then became part of an established policy, the general drift of which was not reversed in 1938. Some outlines of the theory of the subject have been presented in the preceding chapter. Aspects other than effects on the process of economic evolution are irrelevant to our purpose. The quantitative importance of the change to the interests concerned is unquestionable and unquestioned. Hence, we need not go into details or follow up the successive steps embodied in the revenue acts from 1934 to 1937, but can confine ourselves to the following comments.

As the above suggests, the writer is inclined to stress the importance of the income, corporation, and estate taxes at the expense of others which, being novelties, have been more widely discussed. The facts that the limit of exemption from the income tax is very high, the flat rate very low, and the surtax distinctly moderate up to an income of $30,000, are irrelevant to the argument. It is above that range, principally within a group of not more than 30,000 or 40,000 taxpayers that, the structure of American industry being what it is, those taxes, raised within a few years to their present figures, exert a serious influence on "capital supply" and business behavior, which, of course, is greatly intensified by the failure of legislation to permit the carrying forward of business losses, by the new treatment of personal holding companies and by other inroads into actual or potential capital.

The so-called capital gains tax has been held responsible for having accentuated, if not caused, the slump. The writer is, however, unable to see that it can have had much to do with the processes of the current Juglar except by way of damping speculative ardors and thereby making issues of stock more difficult than they would have been. The financing of the positive phase cannot, considering the abundance of cheap money, have been seriously interfered with by this; the subsequent slump should, if anything, have been mitigated by it. Other points, in particular the effect it exerts — not by reducing "oversaving" — but by enforcing dissaving, though relevant to a prognosis of the results to be expected in the future from the capitalist engine and not substantially affected by the modifications introduced by the revenue act of 1938, need not concern us here.

The antisaving theories and the *ressentiments* of the day found a very characteristic expression in the special surtax on undistributed corporate income (undivided profits tax), which ranged from 7 to 27 per cent. Discarding again the question of the long-run effects which the measure might have had if it had been allowed to remain on the statute book, we may split immediate effects into those of a further increase in the burden on corporate income and those of the specific penalty imposed on corporate accumulation, and confine ourselves to the latter. It possibly resulted in an absolute and relative increase in distributed income which is neither certain nor easy

to evaluate because there were also other reasons for the increase that actually occurred, but which, whether great or small, presumably increased, or helped to counteract the decrease of, system expenditure. Nevertheless, the measure may well have had a paralyzing influence on enterprise and investment in general. The actual presence of accumulated "reserves," and the possibility of accumulating them quickly, strengthens the position of a concern with respect to the risks and chances of innovation and expansion which it confronts. One of the causes of the efficiency of private business is that, unlike the politician or public officer, it has to pay for its mistakes. But the consequences of having to do so are very different according to whether it risks owned or borrowed "funds," or whether a loss will only reduce surpluses or directly impinge upon original capital. Adequate book reserves are as necessary a requisite as adequate stocks of raw material, and in their absence, or with reduced facilities of acquiring or replenishing them, an entirely different and much more cautious business policy would impose itself. In prosperity, investment opportunities would be seen in a perspective of reduced proportions; in depression, firms would have to bow more readily to the storm. In the latter case in particular, the important class of considerations — pure business considerations among them — that used to induce many firms "to make a stand" for some time, even at considerable immediate loss, would tend to vanish from the businessman's mind. All this, it is true, vanishes from the economist's mind as soon as he buries himself in the mechanics of aggregative theory. But many industries, which are among the chief economic assets of the nation and of which the automobile industry is the standard instance, would under a regime of undivided profits taxes never have developed as they did. . . .

It should be observed that this is a matter of value of assets and not of liquidity, which under the conditions prevailing in this country since 1931 was never a problem for a concern of unimpaired standing. Similarly, the argument that accumulations make it easier for a concern to live in depression and to "cushion" the effects of depression on the economic process by keeping up dividend and wage payments cannot be met by pointing out that only a part of total accumulations is held in cash or near-cash and that the rest cannot be "paid out." It is true that from the standpoint of the individual management liquidity constitutes an advantage. The ease with which the bulk of American large-scale industry steered through the vicissitudes of 1931 and 1932 was to a considerable extent due to it. It is also true that accumulations which are held in a liquid form tend to work in an anticyclical sense. But this must not be confused with the point which the writer is trying to make and which, in this case, is entirely independent of cash considerations, though it would not be so for other times and countries.

The effect on the combined federal cash account of the method chosen for financing the social security program has been mentioned before. No further attention need, hence, be paid to the money-market and expenditure aspects of the payments into the Old Age Reserve Account and the Unemployment Trust Fund. Independently of this, the tax on pay rolls levied on firms was of course a nonnegligible element in the increase of the total fiscal burden which occurred in 1937. The question of effects raises difficult problems in transference. In a situation in which wage rates are firmly upheld and prices of the products of "big business" not allowed to rise, increase of the tax to the full amount ultimately contemplated may not only produce additional unemployment, but also be sufficient, as comparison with corporate net earnings shows, to cause paralysis in some industries, such as would, for example, enforce the creation of another and much more stringent NRA. But for the time being no major effect can be attributed to this tax taken by itself.

Labor policies reduced investment opportunity — besides employment per unit of output — mainly by forcing up wage rates. We have seen, however, that not all of the increase which actually occurred can be attributed to those policies; and precisely because rising rates were to a considerable extent met by labor-saving rationalization, the effect on investment opportunity was presumably not very great. Costs incident to employing labor were also increased in other ways. And more than elsewhere it is here necessary to define investment opportunity widely and to take account of the less measurable effects of increasing difficulties in operating plants which the growth of a new body of administrative law entails. A major measure of this kind, the National Labor Relations Act (July 5, 1937)[1] was placed on the statute book in the period under survey. As the reader knows, more vigorous use was immediately made of the facilities created by it than is suggested by its actual contents, which keep within the most ordinary lines of labor policy in modern democracies and only develop the principles of earlier legislation, such as the labor clauses of railroad acts, the Clayton Act,

[1] The Act actually was passed on July 5, 1935. [Editor's note.]

certain acts passed during the war, Sec. 7a of the recovery act, and other enactments. Official support given to the campaign of the Committee for Industrial Organization and lending to the act a color not naturally its own, must be listed independently. But after the fullest allowance for these and other elements of the case, we shall still be left with the result that labor policies — more precisely, what has actually been done in the field of labor policy — were not, *taken by themselves,* of decisive importance in shaping the business situations of those years.

As regards what we have called industrial policies unfavorable to investment opportunity — or, what economically amounts to the same thing, to action being taken on any "objective" investment opportunity, whether declining or not, that may have been present — two instances will sufficiently illustrate what we mean. First, . . . developments in the field of public utilities [should have been stronger in the thirties.] The writer does not see how it could possibly be denied that in this case existing investment opportunity was prevented from having its normal effect, not so much by what was actually done, but by the blanket threat behind it. Expected competition from federal or municipal power plants was a factor in some sectors. The Public Utilities Holding Company Act endangered the American solution of the fundamental problem of power finance. But the decisive element of the situation was that indefinite threat: executives and investors would have had to be completely blind to the political forces that were being marshaled against them, if they had been prepared to take the responsibility for, or to cooperate in, new investment on a large scale. The case thus serves to show not only how unrealistic

any theory of investment opportunity is which leaves the political factor out of account, but also how easily the latter may acquire an importance compared with which that of any decline of investment opportunity from reasons inherent to the capitalist process would be negligible, even if it did occur at a significant rate per year.

Second, there is nothing surprising in the fact that under the circumstances the no less old hostility against "monopoly power" should have asserted itself again all over the industrial field. But "monopoly" really means any large-scale business. And since economic "progress" in this country is largely the result of work done within a number of concerns at no time much greater than 300 or 400, any serious threat to the functioning of these will spread paralysis in the economic organism to a much greater degree than a similar threat to the corresponding number of concerns would, in any other country. No compensation was afforded by the federal government's extreme anxiety not to show hostility to private business in general or to do anything that could have aroused the cry of Government in Business, because the contributions of the favored strata to "progress" and their investments are not only comparatively small but also, to a large extent, induced by what happens in the world of big business. That hostility propelled or facilitated the fiscal and labor policies which we have glanced at above. Beyond these very little was actually done; but much was foreshadowed at various times, even before the monopoly investigation, recently instituted. This may have meant nothing or everything, according to whether or not the threats — no doubt, again indefinite — were taken seriously by those who decisions they could have influenced. But it should be observed how very much like "liquidity preference owing to vanishing investment opportunity" the behavior would look which would result if they were.

It will be seen that none of all the *measures* mentioned under our three headings can, if considered individually, be reasonably held to have played a dominant role [during the past few years.] An easy road thus seems to lead toward the conclusion adopted as a matter of fact by many, if not most, economists, that no explanation can on these lines be derived for the lack of vitality displayed by the economic process during the period under survey, and that investment opportunities must, hence, be vanishing from causes internal to that process, in spite of all we have adduced to the contrary. It is, however, suggested that the following considerations greatly strengthen the case for the adequacy of that explanation.

First, the combined effect of a series of measures unfavorable to investment opportunity can evidently not be evaluated by adding up the effects which each of them would have had in the absence of the others. We have repeatedly met cases of this kind. For instance, the reader will recall that our discussion of the course of German wage rates did not result in anything amounting to proof — or rather that it led us to deny — that this element would have spelled serious disturbance if it had acted alone; but that, since it did not, this was not the relevant question to put. Similarly, we might in the case before us make even larger concessions than the writer would be prepared to justify, to the prevalent tendency to underestimate the effects of any or all the individual measures we have glanced at, and nevertheless have to conclude that their combined effects were adequate to produce the observed result.

The individual measures obviously tended to reinforce each other. "Objectively" — *i.e.*, irrespectively of intentions harbored by any individuals — they amounted to systematic attack on investment opportunity all round: it was frontally attacked by direct reduction of revenues — or the operative part of total net revenues — through taxation, which would have been only the more effective if there really had been also an inherent tendency for investment opportunity to shrink; simultaneously, it was attacked in the rear by increasing costs; and both attacks were supplemented by a third — the attack on those traditional methods of management, pricing, and financing in the sphere of "big business" which were associated with the latter's emergence and successes. No doubt, opinions still may in all fairness differ as to the importance both of these combined attacks and of the precise points in the industrial structure that were being attacked. But difference of opinion is not possible about the relevance of the principle of interpretation which the writer is trying to stress.

Second, the mistake involved in trying to arrive at an estimate of combined effects by that process of addition is not more serious than the mistake of confining attention, in evaluating either isolated or combined effects, to the wording of enactments, congressional declarations of policy, and statements of the chief executive. Economists who pride themselves on the practical bent of their researches could really be expected to know that the personnel and methods by which and the spirit in which a measure or set of measures is administrated, are much more important than anything contained in any enactment. We have met with examples above. The events surrounding the National Labor Relations

Act will again serve to illustrate that simple truth, particularly if we compared American with English experience in that field: it should be obvious that in the one case effects on investment opportunity may result which it would be absurd to expect in the other. This already covers part of what we designate by the term Social Atmosphere.

But, third, this atmosphere should also be listed independently as an additional factor in its own right. It is surely not too much to ask economists to realize that behavior in human societies differs from behavior in animal societies or in physical systems, in that it not simply reacts to "disturbances" but to interpretative and anticipative— correct or false — diagnoses of them. Real or supposed drifts and trends may count as much as or more than facts, threats as much as actions, indefinite threats more than specific ones, in creating the psychic environment in which the nation's work has to be done. We know that behind those measures, administrative acts, and anticipations there is something much more fundamental, viz., an attitude hostile to the industrial bourgeoisie which is no ephemeral composite of individual circumstances and political exigencies of the day but the product of the same social process that created that bourgeoisie. Businessmen presumably do not hold that theory. But they need not hold any in order to realize that there is in those measures and programs more than there would have been in similar measures and programs 30 years ago. They are not only, but they feel threatened. They realize that they are on trial before judges who have the verdict in their pocket beforehand, that an increasing part of public opinion is impervious to their point of view, and that any particular indictment will, if successfully met, at

once be replaced by another. Again, we may differ in our estimates of the importance both of this factor and of the functions it tends to paralyze, but it should not be overlooked.

Fourth, the effects of all that on investment opportunity — if the reader prefer, on what to the businessman appears as an investment opportunity of a given degree of attractiveness — were greatly enhanced by the suddenness of the change of scene. In order to convince ourselves of this, it is only necessary to reflect that any major change in the relations between the individual and the state, including any major shift in favor of the latter of the shares in total private revenue earned, involves changes in the fundamental habits of mind, the attitudes to life, and the valuations at least of those who are immediately concerned. The sociology of this need not detain us. But as a matter of history it is clear that such changes usually come about by small installments and as the result of a slow process of education, which must be far advanced for codification of principles into a new body of law to be a success. We observe, in fact, that the modern principles of English taxation took about 30 years to develop and "sink in," and that the beginning of the modern system of English social policies dates back to at least the eighties of the nineteenth century, when the ideas of Chamberlain and Dilke spread dismay among their colleagues in Gladstone's second administration. The English bourgeoisie was thus given time to acclimatize. . . .

But in this country there was no such preparation; hence, there was a different reaction. Barring the war intermezzo, there was nothing except the feeling against "monopolies" and utilities to indicate any resentment, and that was of the middle-class type only and easy to keep in hand. On the whole, the businessman's moral world was the nation's moral world right up to the crisis. And for nearly two years the democratic administration, though doing many things which were felt to be "unorthodox" by its friends as well as by its foes — measures actually were, as we have seen, not so very much out of keeping with American tradition — in no way displayed the attitude that we are discussing now but, on the contrary, signs of a thoroughly bourgeois attitude. The change in policy dates only from 1934–1935. It therefore followed rather than preceded the radicalization of the public mind, which in consequence of the crisis had occurred between 1930 and 1933 as radicalization in countries in which authority is associated with military values will occur in consequence of military defeat.

The analogy with the German breakdown in 1918 suggested by the last remark indicates the line on which we should explain how and why a secular process, after having failed to assert itself to any practically significant extent for fully forty years after the closing of the frontier, then suddenly became the dominant factor of the political situation. In doing so, we should no doubt have to go into many circumstances peculiar to the American environment in general and to American politics in particular, in order to understand the details of the change in attitude and of the resulting political pattern. But the fact, the broad causes, and the effects on business behavior are sufficiently obvious to establish our point without any analysis of details. There are, however, two aspects which cannot be passed by.

On the one hand, we have insisted above on the importance of personnel and of methods of administration. New measures as well as new attitudes must be implemented by a skilled civil service. In any case they set a difficult task to even the most experienced bureaucracy. As a rule, however, reforming governments enjoy at least the advantage of having that indispensable tool ready at hand — in most historical instances it grew up along with the tendencies which they represent. This happened, for example, in England, while in Germany the regime of 1918 was able to take over from its predecessor both an excellent civil service and a state-broken public. In this country a new bureaucracy had suddenly to be created. However good part of the material on which it was necessary to draw, and however creditable, considering the circumstances, the performance of a great many individuals and groups may have been, there was no experience, no *esprit de corps,* no clear idea even of what civil service is and what it can and cannot do. No less inexperienced — to the point of not seeing the fundamental administrative problems at all — were the men in whose hands that unwieldly apparaus was put. The tact, the reserve, the *savoir-faire* which are second nature to a seasoned bureaucracy were alike absent. Enthusiastic individuals and groups developed their own policies and tried to push them with Congress and the public, scornfully refusing counsels of self-denial and patience. In consequence, that sense of indefinite threat was immeasurably increased. English policies may be felt to be equally or more oppressive, but they are never aggressive: spectacular manifestations of aggressiveness proceed only from quarters that are — by *all* parties — firmly held in check, and never from members of the public service. The methods of the latter may be likened to deer-stalking and tend to minimize trouble and disturbance caused by any given measure. Administrative methods in this country tend to maximize them and are more like those of the fox hunt — and this makes a lot of difference.

On the other hand, sudden change, unless of the Russian type, is of necessity imperfect change. It impinges upon a set of economic and political conditions which are very unequally ripe. This puts advocates and opponents of new departures in false positions, adulterates arguments, and makes it impossible to face issues squarely. In England the question of the employment of nonunionized labor, for instance, having been allowed to mature, is now one of secondary importance. In this country it cannot even be frankly put, yet it is at the bottom of much strategy and struggle which, precisely because the issue is not ripe for decision, must be expected to remain for some time a source of difficulties and losses to all parties concerned. But the standard instance is the policy followed with respect to public utilities. Here, if anywhere, there was an all but united public opinion, united at least in its hostility to the private interests involved. Moreover, European experience suggestively pointed toward nationalization of power production and transmission, which could have been carried without any shock to "business confidence" if the interests of investors had been fully safeguarded, and with but a sharp and short one if they had been sacrificed — always provided that there were no clenched fists or indeterminate threats of other nationalizations to follow. Yet it was not even attempted. The clenched fists and indeterminate threats were all the more in evidence, however, and the result was,

as we have seen, to paralyze one force without substituting another. This will always result from raising issues before they can be effectively dealt with and illustrates what above has been described as deadlock. To deny that this impairs the efficiency of the economic engine or, if we retain the slogan, reduces investment opportunity, would seem to the writer unreasonable.

If the above considerations are given their proper weight, there should not be left much doubt as to the adequacy of the factors external to our process to account both for the disappointing features [of the economy's performance since 1933] and for the weakness of the response of the system to government expenditure, in particular for the failure of the latter to affect investment and employment more than it did. It cannot be proved in the sense in which a mathematical theorem can, that the balloon shriveled, not from causes inherent to its structure, but because the air was being sucked out of it. It is, however, highly plausible and, after all only what, if we clear our minds of cant, we should expect to occur in transitional stages. Prognosis would, in this country more than in any other, have to take account of the likelihood that there will be intermissions or even reversals; of the effects of "acclimatization"; and of the fact that, if our schema is to be trusted, recovery and prosperity phases should be more, and recession and depression phases less strongly marked during the next three decades than they have been in the last two. But the sociological drift cannot be expected to change.

III. MODERN INTERPRETATIONS

Ernst W. Swanson: THE FALLACY OF SECULAR STAGNATION

Ernst W. Swanson, now Professor of Economics at North Carolina State College, delivered the following rebuttal of the stagnation thesis as his presidential address before the Southern Economic Association in November 1955. His argument, centering on the creative economic role played by the consumer in Western society, makes outstanding use of psychological insights into a problem in economic analysis.

MANY of you are probably reflecting: Why flog a dead horse, why resurrect a now nearly forgotten quarrel? You say to yourselves: The desperate 1930's are a decade and a half behind us; and our private and public economies have both readjusted to respond to the possibility of another similar decline in the employment of resources.

Then there are those of you who with me are still troubled, perhaps as much as was Macbeth by Banquo's ghost. While we have thought we had stabbed deeply, we have not laid stagnation's ghost. It still hovers around deaf to our defense of these many years past against a thesis which envisaged a maturing of the American economy to the point of stagnation. It haunts us in some of the utterings on the price-parity doctrine and on the guaranteed annual wages; and it takes another form on the other side of the graveyard in the demands for a balanced budget when the Treasury should be showing surpluses. That we did not stab deep enough is quite apparent.

To my knowledge there is no one rational who denies the possibility of a decline of the rate of growth of the private enterprise economy. The quarrel has really raged over the arguments supporting the claim and not the possibility. As for myself, I have never been too happy with the debate over the theory, with either side of it. And I have been most unhappy with the role that I have sought to play. Ever since Lord Keynes sounded the first discordant notes of secular stagnation — notes taken up and built into a crescendo by Alvin Hansen, Oscar Lange, Benjamin Higgins, and numerous others — I have believed the stagnation theory as it developed deficient in certain respects, whose exact form managed to puzzle my poor powers of perception. In casting about for a different background against which to portray my argument, I have shifted my own position in a direction that I find hard to plot.

What I shall attempt to do this evening is to state this position as clearly as my present stage of thinking permits; and I offer the following points for your consideration:

1) the stagnation theory as usually couched fails to join adequately hypothesis and experience and consequently seeks to explain the decline in the rate of growth of the private enterprise economy primarily by forces external to the system;

2) because of their reliance upon a positivis-

From Ernst W. Swanson, "The Economic Stagnation Thesis, Once More," *Southern Economic Journal*, Vol. XXII, 3 (January 1956), pp. 287–304. Reprinted by permission of the *Southern Economic Journal* and of the author.

tic radical behaviorism, the stagnationists deny the individual consumer any part in the determining of economic progress;

3) perforce the stagnationists are committed to the static view upon want satisfaction of the classicists and the temporal dimensions of consumption and its growth are ignored;

4) lacking this understanding of want satisfaction as a process, the stagnationists take but a cursory view of the place of creativity in the explanation of economic progress; and

5) by this failure, they cannot envisage the important function of the consumer as an innovator in his own right and how he has everything to do with economic stagnation and progress.

The Theoretical Obligation of Joining Hypothesis with Experience in the Explanation of Reality as Opposed to the Determinism of the Stagnation Theory

The stagnation theory is offered as an explanation of why the private enterprise economic system suffered severe depression in the 1930's. I believe this explanation oversimplified, to the point where it borders on romanticism. The ideational and conceptual structure of the theory is only hazily sketched and, given this vagueness of structure, somehow or other, the corpus of facts, the products of man's experience with socioeconomic processes, has not been properly marshalled and correlated.

These observations on the theory are not peculiar to it alone. The very classical theory of value and distribution economics, in which the stagnation theory had its methodological roots, did not escape this self-same deficiency. Consider, for example, the form taken by the theories of the Benthamites and the Fabians. But in the stagnation theory the drift towards an extreme point of view has been the greater; the emphasis has been definitely upon the destination of the system rather than upon its direction.

Having its origin, in part in classical economics, the stagnation theory perhaps could not escape the classical view on the nature of economic development: that an economy expands (or contracts) according to a rigid law; and hence what happened in the 1930's was a disruption of the law. The rise of the unemployment of resources as a supposedly long-run phenomenon is to be explained. Employment is construed as a dependent variable, the behavior of which is related in some manner to the accumulation of capital, given the propensity to consume. Unemployment is of course the obverse of employment and is negatively correlated with the changes in capital formation. But capital formation can in turn be affected by various factors, some of which are definitely external to the system: changes in population, technology, and territory (the disappearing frontier).

The explanation, to say the least, is logical and in this respect has much to commend it. But being logical is not a sufficient test of good theory. A logically perfect theory gives us no reason for thinking that it will always survive in the face of a new situation. By adherence to the point of view that it does, the error first committed by the Aristotelians is recommitted; if the law does not explain a situation, the disrupting element is a departure from the law and it cannot be viewed as having rational content. The assumption is that law is rigidly fixed and the nonconforming factor need not be incorporated into the system which the law seeks to explain; it is simply atypical and in itself is therefore a sufficient explanation of the disruption.

Such theorizing is largely implicit and the explanation afforded is incomplete.

Data seem to be used by the stagnation-ists as a picture of reality. Actually, as we acquire more experience with our system, that is, as we gain more and more data having reliability, our possession of it necessitates a reexamination of the system purporting to give reality. Data . . . are antecedent to the acquisition of knowledge about a system; they are set off by themselves. Hence they do not constitute knowledge of the system itself. We cannot stop with the results of our experience, that is, with the data; they must be geared to our hypotheses about the system before we can have an idea about how the system works. Hypotheses reformulated under the accumulating data force upon us the necessity of finding a new reality. Reality is not found in the data alone, not in the hypotheses alone, but in both when properly related to each other. Logic alone gives us nothing but identity; empiricism alone, nothing but phenomenalism. We might go so far as [to say] that the moment a new situation arises, the universal explanation is now no longer universal. The exceptional case has nullified the former meaning attached to the system and the world is no longer rational. It assumes rationality again only when the new problem is solved; in our case, when the disrupting elements are explained and entered into the system.

As usually formulated, the stagnation theory has not reached this level of discourse. We find in it no adequate juncture of hypotheses and empiricism. It relies almost completely on the injection of changed conditions into the system without really developing how this injection is related to human experience, the behavior of the individual consumers and producers who comprise the economic system and who in some way or other respond to stimuli. To no small degree,

it finds reality in the data itself, an identification which scientifically cannot acquire validity until the additional step of joining of empiricism and idea is taken. For the facts in themselves possess a reality which is independent of logic. The failure to recognize this nature of data (and its changes) leads to the substitution of faith for logic, of romanticism for theory.

The stagnation theory thus carries over with it certain serious errors of classical theory; the mechanistic and deterministic colorings particularly stand out. As did the classicists, the stagnationists have worked Newtonian principles of cause and effect into the support of their theoretical system. In a world so conceived, control over the conditions giving rise to a system was assumed operative beyond the administrations of man himself. Man could manipulate and control a system only to the extent that he adhered to the laws governing the behavior of the system. Anything found not consistent with the laws or universals was dubbed irrational and presumably left the system unaffected in the long run.

The Radical Positivistic Bent of the Stagnationists and the Consequent Neglect of Human Behavior in Explaining Economic Change

The relationship between employment and capital formation as usually stated is supposed almost inexorable in its operation. (Consider the assumptions leading to the usual formulations of the shape of the consumption function.) Impacts from the outside upon the system which disturb this operation and affect employment adversely, can be mitigated only through gigantic, persistently continuous undertakings by the public economy. Man is conceived so much a puppet of his environment that for all intents and purposes we may say that his behavior is predetermined by forces beyond his control and he must resort to authority seemingly sometimes beyond him for solution. Economic behavior is thus given such esoteric dimensions that we can almost term the theory so couched animistic.

This view upon man and his economic pursuits and behavior has further classical origins in a social psychology found in the sociology of Herbert Spencer. According to this way of looking at the relationship between mind, nature, and society, man's central nervous system is affected by stimuli from the outside. These stimuli produce such patterns of behavior that in large measure man's self plays only a respondent and not an emergent role.

Of more recent vintage in this kind of psychology, is John Broadus Watson's positivistic radical behaviorism which seems to have a direct kinship to the psychology behind the stagnation theory. By his way of thinking behaviorism is the study of individual experience as it is judged from the individual's conduct and only as it is observed by the psychologist. Also quite definitely oversimplified, this form of behaviorism reflects (1) a denial of the role in an individual's behavior of his private life and (2) particularly, the acceptance of the proposition that the individual's behavior is conditioned by responses to stimuli coming only from the environment surrounding the individual: an extreme form of sociality of the nature of our knowledge about man. In effect, Watson goes so far as to say that even if there were such a thing as the private life of an individual, it is not amenable to scientific observation and, therefore, cannot be offered a place in the explanation of human conduct. Consequently, man is a creature solely of the stimuli external to him. By this

conception, man enjoys neither the power of imagery nor the capacity of consciousness. Here, on the whole, is an unfortunate conclusion for the proper understanding of social behavior.

Man's conduct is far from being this simple, either in form or in origin. Whatever the nature of scientific investigation, observation by any method known to man today cannot be accorded the precision implied in the methodology developed under radical behaviorism. Modern quantum and statistical theories have time and time again demonstrated the correctness of this point of view. The seeking of precision to the point of determinateness, to where it actually obscures behavior, can not only be unproductive of any real understanding of socioeconomic processes, it can in fact be dangerous from the standpoint of public policy.

What is the result of this attitude with its almost anti-intellectual twist is the continuance in force in contemporary socioeconomic thought of the classical notions of what determines progress, economic or otherwise. As I see it, progress is by this way of thinking visualized as a simple process *towards goal set, external to the process of development itself.* Early evidence of this kind of thinking is to be found in the economics of J. S. Mill, Bentham, Marx, and others of that age. Predeterminism is the by-word. We see it in Marx's concept of the final stage of economic development, the dictatorship of the proletariat, whereunder, by a change of economic institutions according to patterns of economic development already laid out, man quite mysteriously would be transformed by the new environment into a creature free of economic strife and conflict. Or we find it in Bentham's utilitarian Utopia, whereunder man by following the universals of social justice as envisaged by Bentham would achieve the ultimate in social order. And so on, to the stagnationists who see a permanent marriage of the private and public economics in some way not fully developed, but with emphasis on the role of the public economy in fostering economic activity — another form of recourse to an authority beyond man himself, the sovereignty of government.

But man is not so easily reconstructed as radical behaviorism would have us believe; nor is he a creature entirely subservient to the whims of forces external to him. Rather — as by Knight's conception — he is a problem-solving animal. Modern man particularly is concerned with the resolution of the difficulties which he is continuously encountering; through his growing understanding of the efficiency of the juncture of logic and empiricism he is affecting this resolution. Externality and the exogenous tend together to disappear in a world so construed, in a world, particularly, where conduct is related to actions growing out of problem-solving or reflective measures. Reality is in the present and not in the past. And the past is not the sole determinant of the present, although the present has emerged from the past.

Any event which takes place cannot really be exhaustively explained "by the conditions of its occurrence." To attempt to do so leads only to an erroneously materialistic concept of both the world and society which has hounded man from Aristotle to modern times. Even more, it leads to identical equations in the description of a system and to a changeless reality, whatever the time under which a system is observed. Here is why man has been relegated into the backdrop of the scene of change and has had supposedly little to do with it. In philosophy, it was not until Alexander, Whitehead, and Mead; and in economics, it

was not until, first, Marshall, Knight, and Schumpeter and, later, Wright and Lundberg, that man was raised to the role of actor and decision-maker that he really had all along played. Through reflective thinking and acting according to ideas formulated by him, man's part in socioeconomic processes is made definitely positive.

The present, by Mead's and Whitehead's ways of looking at it, is always in someway unique and new, "something which is not completely determined by the past and out of which it rose." The present contains within its characteristic of temporal and causal discontinuity. (Hence, the relationship between the variations in employment and investment may not entirely be what it seems to be.) New things emerge and, as they emerge, they do not follow from the past in the predetermined fashion of the classicists. *The past cannot possibly be made to hold the new in its entirety.* To be sure, after the new has emerged, we seek to reconstruct our experience according to its emergence, through either our contactual and/or distant relationship to it. Forthwith we change our interpretation of the past and try to conceive of it as something which participated in the emergence of the present. Classical thinkers could but give place to the past; modern thinkers must recognize both the past and the future. The future is found in the ideas we develop about it. In reconstructing the place of the past in the present, we create a new set of universals or laws and on their application to the present we acquire an understanding of how the conditions of the present come about. Mead holds that there are experiences and data which can possess importance only because they are the property of a given individual. To be sure, these individual experiences eventually may affect others measurably. Because the universal, the opposite of the individual, is not forever fixed and unchangeable, the given experience of an individual can become a part of the experience of the many. Thus, the atypical individual himself by affecting the progress of society may effect the reconstruction of a universal, a theory, or even an institution. Consider the impact which Jesus and Aristotle have had upon the Western world.

To assume a definite, determinate past to which everything in the present must conform amounts to the denial of the new and of the possibility of the emergence of the present. At the same time, to treat the new as wholly alien to the past is to put it in the realm of mysticism. The present is a juncture of the past and the new; a juncture of conformance and of nonconformance; and, in ideas, the twice-told and the just discovered. Man, as an intellectual, reflective creature, is capable of ideation. Man is therefore able to see beyond the past and the present and to create the novel. Contrary to the heritage from Spencer and Watson, man can select among different ideas and among different stimuli which appear to him. "Not only do we open the door to creative stimuli and close it to others, but our attention is an organizing process as well as a selective process. . . . Our attention enables us to organize the field in which we are going to act. Here we have the organism as acting and determining its environment."

Man in reality is both "I" and "me." The "me" is the organized attitudes of society which we take on in assuming the role of the other man; we seek to see ourselves "as others see us." The "me" limits the behavior of the individual, the "I." But the "I" asserts itself within these limits and contributes to change and to reconstruction of ideas. The modern personality is a powerful juncture of the "I"

and the "me." In primitive societies and in societies which have "matured" and settled to the paths tread by its forebears, the individual self is determined solely by the patterns of the groups to which it belongs. In the highly progressive society, the "I" stands out and the "me" is pushed into the background; the "me" continues to "control" caprice, but the more advanced society is, the more forceful is the "I." Individuals who are "endowed" particularly with new ideas break through the circular, confining forces of traditionalism and rise above the past, and through their introduction of the novel tend to pull others with them. *Progress and stagnation are the products of human conduct and not of external forces.* Every individual, every generation of a progressive society recomposes its history. The process of rise and decline of a civilization is a two-way street; we are affected by our environment *but in turn we reconstruct it.*

The appearance of a system in which the individual self, the "I," can operate is therefore far from circular in development; and it may not even be linear. The system develops through conflicts of ideas and the future is truly an idea of what might be were such or such done. It is indeterminate in some unmeasurable degree. This much we may venture to propose as summary: Minimize the "I" and maximize the "me," we then tend to generate stagnation; maximize the "I" and minmize the "me," we then tend to generate progress.

Want Satisfaction as a Temporal Process and the Stagnationists' Error in Their Identification of Object and Satisfaction

Man is neither driven nor manipulated by forces external to him. He himself transforms his wants into anticipated satisfactions which prompt him to act and to visualize new potentials; and, in acting, he creates new values, new wants, and new economic situations.

The actual occurrence of a want satisfaction is an event to him as an individual. Contact with a means of want satisfaction (the means may be regarded as assets to the individual) is transformed into a feeling of satisfaction as a passing situation for him; indeed, an event of satisfaction has within itself a passage of feeling. In contrast with a means or object of satisfaction, events extend over one another.

The means of satisfaction possess characteristics which exist beyond the event of satisfaction. They are permanent relative to the events of satisfaction which lap over into other events and which do not recur; the characteristics broadly speaking do recur. Thus, the general characteristics of an automobile may be permanent and certainly self-identical. Yet, this permanence is relative since the automobile's situation in the several related events of want satisfaction is changing. In time, when the events of want satisfaction, which also can only be relative to a given situation, have changed to the extent that they no longer afford a conception of the same situation then the automobile leaves or "egresses"; and some other means more approximate to the new but related situation of the want for transportation enters or "ingresses." Hence, the want satisfaction process is over time a continuous ingress and egress of events which never really recur. Only the characteristics of a means possess the property of recurrence and they in association with a given situation render for us the attributes by which we make our choices among means (or assets).

The individual consumer can make a rational choice only through a comparison of events relative to the attributes of the means. But, by inference, the stagnationists identify want satisfaction with a particular object and thus are guilty of the worse kind of identification, the result of adherence to classical logic. Thus, we speak of satisfaction of hunger. Or, we say that we desire the satisfactions which may come from transportation from one place to another. But the automobile, again for example, can never be more than a means to satisfaction although we economists often speak of wanting automobiles. That kind of identification is the classical confusion of object with function — and by function I mean the effects had or achieved.

Satisfaction is at its best a feeling, a process of feeling which is never wholly determinate as to either its intensity or time. The conditions under which each of us "live" and the symbols which we attach to want-satisfying means govern our individual responses; these conditions and symbols are hardly constant! Symbols are mental constructs, devices of language or image which represent a means of satisfaction. They are the instrumentalities by which man sizes up a given means of satisfaction and they excite his perceiving of the attributes of the means. They are in themselves nonphysical and they are a phase of experience and are both social and emergent. The actual sensations derived from a contact with an object are not physical. The symbols which are attached to an object through the observation of the sensations, now construed as data, enter into a cognitive act of the mind, and a solution to the problem of choice among alternatives is required.

Progress and Creativity — a Fundamental Relationship Unobserved by the Stagnationists

Man's experience is especially colored by his efforts to resolve all present dissatisfactions. This effort applies especially to economic experience. Vacua in his experience stir him into action and into planning for that action; the process of choosing is relatively continuous. Man seeks harmony, unity of action and purpose. Only in the case of man and, to date, Western man, do new patterns of activity therefore arise as ends. Every task of man is really a matter of change, a process of learning or re-learning. The result is change in both his attitude and symbol.

Such a process is always achieving a result, something new is added and something already achieved is discarded. Whitehead would say nothing can be absolutely new, nor can it be absolutely old. What is accomplished borrows a bit from the past, a bit from the present, and a bit from the future. The process is more than a simple coming-to-pass. It results in definite events of satisfaction. These events are actual and represent the process in as nearly a quantitative manner as can be approximated. They really come into existence and pass out of existence in a causal sequence.

In classical economics wants are stated as given. This assumption of givenness leads to the exclusion of the process of creativity inherent in the want satisfaction process of Western man. Marshall long ago appropriately reflected that value as a consideration of what is to be chosen cannot be treated apart from activity; and where there is no activity there is really nothing much else. In a stationary world, where flows or goods are at constant rates of the same goods on end, resources would be allocated by an accepted and unchanging pattern. No one would actually have to make an economic decision, nor make economic plans. Activity in the sense of problem-solving would be reduced to the barest possible minimum. Value would come to have a meaning different from that of a dynamic world in which there is creativity; value in a stationary world could arise only in conjunction with a comparison of absolutes.

The essence of the Western world, however, is creativeness. It is at the opposite end of the pole from the caste and traditionalistic societies of India and China. In the Western world new wants are constantly arising but in a traditionalistic world want satisfaction is static. Hence, if we take a static view upon the theory of consumption we arrive at pretty much the same kind of conclusion as traditionalists would. An element of the traditionalistic view is carried over into contemporary consumption theory; wants are "created" with the appearance of new goods and services. That construction really places the cart before the horse. Wants and the act of maximization of satisfactions are in themselves creative of an intensity of feeling which engenders the seeking of the new on a broad scale, not necessarily on the part of every individual but certainly on the part of many who seek solutions to their dissatisfactions.

In our Western society, there is something in a great many of us, conceivably the quality of imagination and perspective, which prompts us to seek the new. While all behavior may be said to have social and symbolic dimensions, each individual makes his own contribution to a problem solution. In taking action towards this end an individual changes in some degree the *status quo*. That action is direct. What we think of in a creative sense depends upon our symbols and our backgrounds, the conditions under which we think and act. The emergence of new wants is a matter of degree, usually; but when the area of thinking is reorganized the new is anticipated. The conceptual and symbolic framework determines considerably the extent to which our thinking is creative of the new. Characteristically, Western man not only seizes upon the new, but goes out of his way to develop or create the new. He wants more than what he has now; "more," particularly in the sense of something beyond the mere repetition of what is already in existence. In a word, the tendency of an individual act of want satisfaction is to initiate a process of fulfillment which in turn seeks higher fulfillment or satisfaction, *ad infinitum*.

* * *

Man's concern in a dynamic society is, therefore, not maximization of utility under *given wants* but maximization under *wants which are creatively advancing and are made creative by the very efforts to maximize*. We are indeed primarily concerned with the reorganizing of the means of want satisfaction which will yield the greatest possible *growth* of satisfaction. *The very process of maximizing partakes of a creative element, for in order to maximize want satisfaction we must make those decisions about the use of resources which we expect to lead us to our goals, and in making them we develop an awareness of and desire for the higher qualities of things.* We give thought to both quantity and quality. Intensity of feeling is a function of these two elements. *Hence wants are "caused" to change under the process of maximization.*

In the feelings that have been occasioned through the evolvement of, say, television, a certain intensity of satisfaction has been reached. That intensity in turn becomes the data for a new occasion. New feelings emerge. In time they take on a new intensity and there is creation of a new occasion of satisfaction. Creativity is thus a process of bringing together various means of satisfaction into new unities of feelings of satisfaction. Here is the very essence of progress.

The Consumer as an Innovator and His Role in the Determination of Economic Stagnation and Progress

The concept of creativity suggests that the contemporary formulation of the stagnation theory rests upon a tacit assumption about a fixed standard of living for each income decile. The thesis is the product of (1) the emphasis upon the physical aspects of economic organization and (2) the adoption of the static postulates of classical economics. The truly dynamic qualities of economic growth are ignored.

If we admit that our economic community is a multitude of individuals having ends which engender processes of want satisfaction in a non-traditionalistic way, then under certain conditions almost every individual may be a potential entity of creativity. His rational behavior is directed towards "maximization" in the large of his want satisfaction and thus a cumulative improvement of his asset position is involved.

Every individual possesses sense data against which he achieves his maximization (which includes his cumulative improvement). These sense data, while complex, none the less play a role in explaining his behavior. In contemporary writing there is an overemphasis of the demonstrative effects in behavior. In the real world not all individuals are imbued exclusively with Veblenian tendencies; in fact, most consumers usually desire that some elements of their consumption pattern be distinctive. They prefer to be at least partly independent in their tastes, and to the extent that there is independence to that extent the action of the individual gives a special quality to his

collection or constellation of want-satisfying means.

For individuals with low incomes and
with planes of living below the standards
of decent or contemplated living, both of
which enter into their perspectives, hori-
zons, and plans, the marginal propensity
to consume is usually high and may be
even greater than one. For individuals
with high incomes and planes of living
equal to at least the contemplated standards, the propensity to consume at the
margin is likely to be less than one, given
the income and given the standard. But
for all individuals there are frequent occasions when it is likely that, *as their
sights and/or income expectations are
raised*, the propensity to consume at the
margin closely approaches one or even
exceeds one.

The usual construction of the propensity to consume as found in contemporary analysis must rest on the assumption
that the standards are *absolute and fixed*.
Such analysis is set into a strictly static
setting. Moreover, it has no temporal
value in so far as it concerns judgments
about either a mature or a progressive
(or for that matter a regressive) economy. The hypothesis thus implied leads
to no more than a construction of a
model in which the economy is geared to
consumption and consumption is given
non-temporal qualities. It is inevitable
that the marginal propensity to consume
must be construed as less than one.

The general argument has validity only
when it can be held (1) that the force
of creativity has been virtually dampened, (2) that there is no variability in
the propensity to consume among income
classes and, therefore, relatively no differences in the occurrence of the peaks of
satisfaction among the different income
groups, and (3) that the asset values of
the consuming units are constant.

Consider (1), first: creativity has been
dampened. The proponents of the mature economy thesis must believe particularly that previous satisfactions do not
become the data for the seeking of new
satisfactions. Yet, as we have seen, that
condition has been applicable to only the
Oriental world. For Western man seeks
the highest possible intensity of satisfaction. Creativity is widespread and is the
truly essential force behind the course of
economic growth. It gives rise to relatively continuous changes of a secular
nature of both the plane and standard of
living. Neither should be treated as static
concepts and, given the societal setting
favorable to the operation of creativity,
both would tend to advance over time.

(2) The assumption that, there is no
variability in the propensity to consume
among income classes, ignores the presence of a dynamic element internal to the
consumption function. Usually, the function is formulated without consideration
of the change which may take place in
the propensity to consume over the time.
For the low income groups there are always the pressures of wanting, even as
incomes rise, as standards (goals) of living change with expectations and the
planes of living (achieved goals) are advanced to meet new standards. Some
income groups may achieve a planned
standard of living for the time being and
thus a new level of intensity of satisfaction is engendered. Concurrently, some
never even sight the goals which they
have in view. In the short run, the con-
stituency of these groups is forever
changing so that it is doubtful that the
groups with satisfaction achieved balance
out those who have not reached their
peaks of satisfaction. Therefore, the propensity to consume may be highly variable, even though the general level of
income may be stable.

(3) The assumption that asset values of consumers are constant, ignores the possibility that under relatively progressive conditions the creativity process tends to increase the values of existing assets in total. For as new assets are acquired by the consumer the usefulness of all his assets increases and, accordingly, their total value. This process also contributes to a dissatisfaction with some existing assets and the individual seeks to improve his values by replacing them with assets of higher value. To be sure, at low income levels individuals must fairly consistently pursue past patterns of expenditure. Yet that pattern is far from as rigid as some maintain. Those with low incomes respond almost spontaneously to any rise in income or income expectations.

This last emendation of course has been made explicitly by some neo-Keynesians. Naturally, the proposals to reallocate national income to low income groups through taxation and government spending rest on the assumption that consumers with higher propensities to consume are given an opportunity to spend with the result that additional real income would be generated. It is Duesenberry's contention, moreover, that the propensity to consume of a household is some function, not of the absolute level of its real income, but of its position in the deciles of income, with incomes arrayed in order of magnitude. Therefore, individuals in the low income deciles are discontent and seek to achieve levels of consumption expenditures comparable to those in the income deciles above theirs.

But the proposition advanced here goes beyond these arguments. Both Duesenberry's and the neoKeynesian views are largely colored by classical thinking on consumption. The classicists, as a rule, assumed primarily that new wants tended to displace old. Under some circumstances this view is essentially correct. But there are such relations of wants which lead less often to displacement than to (1) supplementation through complimentarity of new wants to the old and (2) to augmentation, through the addition of new wants to the existing structure. This combined effect gives rise to broad rather than narrow structural changes in wants and, hence, in the asset constellations of individuals.

The preference for consumption goods is thus creatively delineated. It involves choice not in a static but in a dynamic sense, for purpose is inherently dynamic. The individual holds before him a standard of living that is usually higher than his plane of living. Under dynamic considerations, as shown above, want-satisfying activity becomes a process. As process, it must be distinguished from the degree of intensity of satisfaction and, especially, the highest degree of this intensity. In the usual discussion of maximization problems it is the last construct upon which emphasis is placed. The consumer adds units of goods until the additional items of effect equality of all the marginal utilities or of the marginal rates of substitution of expenditure; and, for the individual, given his real income, total utility is maximized. Nevertheless, process and degree of satisfaction are distinct categories of analysis, even though closely related. Process is especially significant since it dictates the shifts in the parameters; but not in the autonomous sense implied by Duesenberry. These shifts are fairly continuous over time and arise out of human behavior so that the parameters have both spatial and temporal dimensions.

To some extent the position here is a refinement of Duesenberry's. But it goes beyond the point of refinement and suggests that the demonstrative effects are not the sole determinants of behavior. Rather each individual finds or feels something new in what has just happened and he accordingly acts to change his want structure and, therefore, his asset constellation. Some individuals *must* originate new wants and many do; and it is also conceivable that this quality of originality is widely dispersed.

We might go so far as to contend that the instability of income levels is probably largely a reflection of the "maximizing" and creative activity of individuals and households. As want structures change so income levels as a process of interaction change; in turn, this process may even become self-sustaining. Actually, to nearly all individuals or households income is almost always too low, relatively to purpose (standards). Indeed, as a dynamic element, real income is almost always falling, again relatively to purpose, whatever the income class. In spite of rising asset values, it may be falling in the sense that as individuals raise their sights they automatically reduce the value of their real income.

It is at this point in the argument that Whitehead's doctrine especially applies. As compared with other forms of life, human beings are highly complex organisms. Only man is capable of complex feelings about satisfaction (or dissatisfaction) garnered from experience; *only complex organisms enjoy the intensity of feeling which ensues from the choice of activity or from the enjoyment of new patterns of activity.* This capacity to cherish new, heretofore unrealized, ends regenerates and generates change in the structure of wants.

With reference to the influence of other consuming units upon an individual's consumption behavior — the demonstrative effect — the relation among individual consuming units is more complex than what Duesenberry appears to believe to be the case. Actually, consumer's choice is governed not only by these influences but also by each individual's feelings about his experiences. To deny this proposition essentially amounts to a denial that the individual is a thinking organism and has independency of feeling — definitely a reflection of the influence of positivistic radical behaviorism. The idea of interdependence of wants can be carried to the same extreme as did the classicists in their assumption of independence of wants. It should be evident that had there not been a high degree of independence of choice of consuming units there would never had been any need for the complex economic organization of the private or exchange enterprise economy; fairly primitive organizations would have sufficed.

In the modern theory of cosmology the results are greater than the cause; in the realm of human wants the process of creativity leads to an expansion of wants. To use the adjective "quality," as does Duesenberry in the delineation of the factors affecting consumption, implies too much that change involves purely existing things, rather than the creation of new things. His interpretation of behavior is thus extremely narrow. Contrary to what would be his description of its want-satisfying capacity, the automobile, when it came into being, led to more than a simple qualitative change of the want structure. It created an entirely new set of values which in turn led to further creativity and, hence, to new and additional wants. But values and feelings are really identical and by their identification we introduce an important spatial consideration into the argument.

That there is a systematic relationship

between income increases and the propensity to consume, and between increases in the values of assets and the propensity to consume should by now be clear. The rise in income is associated with advances attributable to creativity and, similarly, the values of existing assets are supplemented and complimented by creativity and they also advance. Thus, in our society there is inherent in the propensity to consume a long-run tendency to increase at the margin and on the average. Short-run stability of the propensity to consume may be almost impossible because of the income-generating effects of want-satisfying activities.

That creativity has been on the increase since the turn of this century is an hypothesis seemingly of some validity. Therefore, it is conceivable that since then there may have been a gradual rise in the level of propensity to consume, an upward shift in the function, and in the slope especially. The tremendous increase in the production of consumption goods, qualitywise and quantitywise, is offered as evidence. Consider the percentage rise in the production of consumer durable goods. Completely new developments in wants and want satisfaction had their beginning with the automobile and the home application of electricity, both of them reaching practical application in the first decade of this century. More recently, new materials, plastics, artificial fibres, non-ferrous metals, and forest products have added to this impetus.

In no small way these changes have come about not only because the consumer has been receptive to them, but in some measure — probably highly significant — he has through his search for the new made it possible for entrepreneurial groups to assume the risks surrounding the application of new ideas and techniques. The entrepreneurs are the innovators at one level: they form new combinations of productive agents — Schumpeter's interpretation of their function as innovators. Consumers are innovators at a different level: they inspire and induce entrepreneurs to produce new things by creating an atmosphere amenable to innovation. As in the case of traditionalistically oriented societies, without such atmosphere the entrepreneurial function would evaporate or even fail to develop. Under a private enterprise economy, the entrepreneurs derive an important degree of security from the consumer's role as one kind of innovator.

While usually a proper procedure for analytical purposes, separation here of these two levels of innovation results in the wrong interpretation of the position of the consumer in the production and investment process. Want satisfaction as a process cannot be separated from other economic processes. Experiences are inseparable from the totality of experiences; to view them separately leads to strictly mechanical and highly positivistic interpretations of consumer behavior. Only a narrow construction of consumption or of production is obtained. Traditionalistic organization of production reflects largely the positivistic interpretation. *In much this same sense, the stagnation theory, as usually derived, is forced to stand upon a narrow interpretation of consumer behavior. Its constructions of the experiences of the consumer are so circumscribed that it fails to admit into its considerations creativity as a characteristic of the consumer of our modern complex society. It is therefore forced in its explanation to recur to exogenous "causes" which have little if any relationship to the realm of consumer experiences. It can only focus attention upon what might be termed the physical or non-behavioral aspects of growth: changes in technology, population, and territory.* This view upon the determinants of growth is centered around relatively fixed elements having only minor validity in the explanation of stagnation; and it has a striking kinship to the Schoolmen's view on nature, that man is bound forever within an environment upon which he has no influence: "The earth and other planets revolve over the same paths from now on until doomsday." All activities become subject to a given and unchanging order.

It might of course be argued that technology is a first cousin to creativity. But it needs to be seen that technology is a by-product of creativity which comes first in the order of things. Creativity may take the form of strictly disinterested curiosity or it may be directed towards the achievement of fairly specific ends; but whatever the form it takes it still comes first. The physical elements of growth are only surface elements.

In both classical and stagnation economics change is really predetermined. "Cause and effect" relations are largely given through the postulates. Nothing creative in content is entered in the "solution." The elements are largely permanently existent; and, as it were, the concern is basically with conservation of energy. But in the real economic world, broadly speaking, it seems quite necessary to go beyond postulates of this nature. *It is necessary in fact to examine man's problem-solving activities under conditions where change is independent of the order of things; self-continuing change is of the essence. Change is thus to be viewed as occurring in an area of endless possibilities of order.* In this sense it becomes indeterminate. This is the exact point on which the classicists and the stagnationists both seem to stub their

respective toes. There is what Cohen has called "the systematic ignoring of possibility and hence . . . a tragically systematic impoverishment of the conception of human nature."

By our interpretation, change acquires a new kind of continuity; not cyclical in essence, though in appearance. Instead it embodies a power of continuation not given the order of things in the traditional sense. Changes, therefore, are not to be regarded as a sign of instability, they are instead an ever-reaching towards greater fulfillment. There is further creation after adoption of the new, on and on, as each new entity is achieved.

The various emphases on the physical elements of growth are limiting in their assessment of the nature of economic development. More embracing is the broader view that there are other elements which enter into economic development: (1) above all, man's creativity and the effect of it upon his wants and his asset structure; and (2) the institutional nature of man's environment, the setting for his creative behavior. The first element is clearly not limiting upon expansion.

Institutional elements need not necessarily be limiting, and up to now they have not been. What they are in effect depends on what man is in body and mind. To the degree that he emphasizes the "I" and imparts flexibility to the systematic group of conditions upon his actions in his social and political environment to that degree he reduces the limiting effects. To the extent that man emphasizes the "me" and seeks to impose a rigid systematic group of conditions upon his behavior to that extent they become limiting.

Indeed, far greater limiting or stagnating effects may arise from the institutional elements when couched in terms of a rigid systematic group of conditions, than from changes in population and technology, which may have only a secondary effect in that conceivably their operation is from the very first conditioned by the institutional elements. By taking essentially this point of view, such critics of the strictly stagnationist position as Fellner, Simons, Schumpeter and Wright, have made a strong point. It appears from their arguments that the physical elements have only a relatively minor validity in the explanation of economic maturity or stagnation. Of far more importance is the socio-political setting; if there is a slow-down of economic growth, it will be for the reason that man has acted politically contrary to his interest, its direction and its intensity.

The direction and intensity of economic development at all times are surrounded by uncertainty. Economic development is by no means the determinate relation usually supposed in contemporary writings on the subject. There are several reasons for this uncertainty but the institutional setting probably accounts for the greatest portion of it. Changes in the setting may lead to serious declines in the rates of acquisition of assets by both consumer and entrepreneur.

Today, there is a growing tendency throughout the Western world for many consumers to identify themselves with various producer groups which are organized for the purposes of "controlling" prices and output and to prevent changes in production methods and in consumption habits. As I have written elsewhere:

The drift is toward group action and group motivation. Wants are more and more dominated by group standards, the latter colored by individual behavior to preserve rather than to advance position. Productive effort is more and more dominated by group standards intended to compress individuals into fairly comparable molds of behavior. . . .

The economy thus departs significantly from the fairly atomistic order of two or three generations ago. It becomes a blend of group and individual behavior and, to borrow Whitehead's term, it takes on some of the characteristics of an "organism." The individuals and groups are differently motivated. Consumption, spending, saving, and investment are differently affected, as structure and institutions change.

The activities of these dominant groups may in fact eventually become so highly purposive to the individual members of such groups that they may substitute group activities, largely sociopolitical in nature, for the usual want-satisfying activities of the individual. Group behavior in contemporary France and Italy comes to mind. *The greater the degree to which this substitution takes place the less is the emphasis upon acquisition of many kinds of consumer assets. The "me" comes to dominate over the "I." Custom and tradition may then largely guide the consumer in his plants and purchases; and creativity is sublimated.* It is then that stagnation truly rears its unsightly head.

John Kenneth Galbraith: THE GREAT STOCK MARKET CRASH
SMASHES AN UNSOUND ECONOMY

Professor of Economics at Harvard since 1942, John Kenneth Galbraith is the author of three celebrated analyses of the postwar economy, American Capitalism, The Affluent Society, *and* The New Industrial State. *Although in the following selection he appears to accept the thesis that the depression represented a failure of investment and growth, he places greater emphasis than other modern writers upon the contribution of institutional and other structural weaknesses to that failure.*

AFTER the Great Crash came the Great Depression which lasted, with varying severity, for ten years. In 1933, Gross National Product (total production of the economy) was nearly a third less than in 1929. Not until 1937 did the physical volume of production recover to the levels of 1929, and then it promptly slipped back again. Until 1941 the dollar value of production remained below 1929. Between 1930 and 1940 only once, in 1937, did the average number unemployed during the year drop below eight million. In 1933 nearly thirteen million were out of work, or about one in every four in the labor force. In 1938 one person in five was still out of work.

It was during this dreary time that 1929 became a year of myth. People hoped that the country might get back to twenty-nine; in some industries or towns when business was phenomenally good it was almost as good as in twenty-nine; men of outstanding vision, on occasions of exceptional solemnity, were heard to say that 1929 "was no better than Americans deserve."

On the whole, the great stock market crash can be much more readily explained than the depression that followed it. And among the problems involved in assessing the causes of depression none is more intractable than the responsibility to be assigned to the stock market crash. Economics still does not allow final answers on these matters. But, as usual, something can be said.

As already so often emphasized, the collapse in the stock market in the autumn of 1929 was implicit in the speculation that went before. The only question concerning that speculation was how long it would last. Sometime, sooner or later, confidence in the short-run reality of increasing common stock values would weaken. When this happened, some people would sell, and this would destroy the reality of increasing values. Holding for an increase would now become meaningless; the new reality would be falling prices. There would be a rush, pellmell, to unload. This was the way past speculative orgies had ended. It was the way the end came in 1929. It is the way speculation will end in the future.

We do not know why a great speculative orgy occurred in 1928 and 1929. The long accepted explanation that credit was easy and so people were impelled to borrow money to buy common stocks on margin is obviously nonsense. On

From John Kenneth Galbraith, *The Great Crash, 1929,* pp. 173–193. Reprinted by permission of Houghton Mifflin Company and of Hamish Hamilton Ltd.

numerous occasions before and since credit has been easy, and there has been no speculation whatever. Furthermore, much of the 1928 and 1929 speculation occurred on money borrowed at interest rates which for years before, and in any period since, would have been considered exceptionally astringent. Money, by the ordinary tests, was tight in the late twenties.

Far more important than rate of interest and the supply of credit is the mood. Speculation on a large scale requires a pervasive sense of confidence and optimism and conviction that ordinary people were meant to be rich. People must also have faith in the good intentions and even in the benevolence of others, for it is by the agency of others that they will get rich. In 1929 Professor Dice observed: "The common folks believe in their leaders. We no longer look upon the captains of industry as magnified crooks. Have we not heard their voices over the radio? Are we not familiar with their thoughts, ambitions, and ideals as they have expressed them to us almost as a man talks to his friend?" Such a feeling of trust is essential for a boom. When people are cautious, questioning, misanthropic, suspicious, or mean, they are immune to speculative enthusiasms.

Savings must also be plentiful. Speculation, however it may rely on borrowed funds, must be nourished in part by those who participate. If savings are growing rapidly, people will place a lower marginal value on their accumulation; they will be willing to risk some of it against the prospect of a greatly enhanced return. Speculation, accordingly, is most likely to break out after a substantial period of prosperity, rather than in the early phases of recovery from a depression. Macaulay noted that between the Restoration and the Glorious Revolution Englishmen were at loss to know what to do with their savings and that the "natural effect of this state of things was that a crowd of projectors, ingenious and absurd, honest and knavish, employed themselves in devising new schemes for the employment of redundant capital." Bagehot and others have attributed the South Sea Bubble to roughly the same causes. In 1720 England had enjoyed a long period of prosperity, enhanced in part by war expenditures, and during this time private savings are believed to have grown at an unprecedented rate. Investment outlets were also few and returns low. Accordingly, Englishmen were anxious to place their savings at the disposal of the new enterprises and were quick to believe that the prospects were not fantastic. So it was in 1928 and 1929.

Finally, a speculative outbreak has a greater or less immunizing effect. The ensuing collapse automatically destroys the very mood speculation requires. It follows that an outbreak of speculation provides a reasonable assurance that another outbreak will not immediately occur. With time and the dimming of memory, the immunity wears off. A recurrence becomes possible. Nothing would have induced Americans to launch a speculative adventure in the stock market in 1935. By 1955 the chances are very much better.

As noted, it is easier to account for the boom and crash in the market than to explain their bearing on the depression which followed. The causes of the Great Depression are still far from certain. A lack of certainty, it may also be observed, is not evident in the contemporary writing on the subject. Much of it tells what went wrong and why with marked firmness. However, this paradoxically can itself be an indication of uncertainty.

When people are least sure they are often most dogmatic. We do not know what the Russians intend, so we state with great assurance what they will do. We compensate for our inability to foretell the consequences of, say, rearming Germany by asserting positively just what the consequences will be. So it is in economics. Yet, in explaining what happened in 1929 and after, one can distinguish between explanations that might be right and those that are clearly wrong.

A great many people have always felt that a depression was inevitable in the thirties. There had been (at least) seven good years; now by an occult or biblical law of compensation there would have to be seven bad ones. Perhaps, consciously or unconsciously, an argument that was valid for the stock market was brought to bear on the economy in general. Because the market took leave of reality in 1928 and 1929, it had at some time to make a return to reality. The disenchantment was bound to be as painful as the illusions were beguiling. Similarly, the New Era prosperity would some day evaporate; in its wake would come the compensating hardship.

There is also the slightly more subtle conviction that economic life is governed by an inevitable rhythm. After a certain time prosperity destroys itself and depression corrects itself. In 1929 prosperity, in accordance with the dictates of the business cycle, had run its course. This was the faith confessed by the members of the Harvard Economic Society in the spring of 1929 when they concluded that a recession was somehow overdue.

Neither of these beliefs can be seriously supported. The twenties by being comparatively prosperous established no imperative that the thirties be depressed. In the past, good times have given way to less good times and less good or bad to good. But change is normal in a capitalist economy. The degree of regularity in such movements is not great, though often thought to be. No inevitable rhythm required the collapse and stagnation of 1930–40.

Nor was the economy of the United States in 1929 subject to such physical pressure or strain as the result of its past level of performance that a depression was bound to come. The notion that the economy requires occasional rest and resuscitation has a measure of plausibility and also a marked viability. During the summer of 1954 a professional economist on President Eisenhower's personal staff explained the then current recession by saying that the economy was enjoying a brief (and presumably well-merited) rest after the exceptional exertions of preceding years. In 1929 the labor force was not tired; it could have continued to produce indefinitely at the best 1929 rate. The capital plant of the country was not depleted. In the preceding years of prosperity, plant had been renewed and improved. In fact, depletion of the capital plant occurred during the ensuing years of idleness when new investment was sharply curtailed. Raw materials in 1929 were ample for the current rate of production. Entrepreneurs were never more eupeptic. Obviously if men, materials, plant, and management were all capable of continued and even enlarged exertions a refreshing pause was not necessary.

Finally, the high production of the twenties did not, as some have suggested, outrun the wants of the people. During these years people were indeed being supplied with an increasing volume of goods. But there is no evidence that their desire for automobiles, clothing, travel, recreation, or even food was sated. On the contrary, all subsequent evidence showed (given the income to spend) a capacity for a large further increase in consumption. A depression was not needed so that people's wants could catch up with their capacity to produce.

What, then, are the plausible causes of the depression? The task of answering can be simplified somewhat by dividing the problem into two parts. First there is the question of why economic activity turned down in 1929. Second there is the vastly more important question of why, having started down, on this unhappy occasion it went down and down and down and remained low for a full decade.

As noted, the Federal Reserve indexes of industrial activity and of factory production, the most comprehensive monthly measures of economic activity then available, reached a peak in June. They then turned down and continued to decline throughout the rest of the year. The turning point in other indicators — factory payrolls, freight-car loadings, and department store sales — came later, and it was October or after before the trend in all of them was clearly down. Still, as economists have generally insisted, and the matter has the high authority of the National Bureau of Economic Research, the economy had weakened in the early summer well before the crash.

This weakening can be variously explained. Production of industrial products, for the moment had outrun consumer and investment demand for them. The most likely reason is that business concerns, in the characteristic enthusiasm of good times, misjudged the prospective increase in demand and acquired larger inventories than they later found they needed. As a result they curtailed their buying, and this led to a cutback in production. In short, the summer of 1929 marked the beginning of the familiar inventory recession. The proof is not conclusive from the (by present standards)

limited figures available. Department store inventories, for which figures are available, seem not to have been out of line early in the year. But a mild slump in department store sales in April could have been a signal for curtailment.

Also there is a chance — one that students of the period have generally favored — that more deep-seated factors were at work and made themselves seriously evident for the first time during that summer. Throughout the twenties production and productivity per worker grew steadily: between 1919 and 1929, output per worker in manufacturing industries increased by about 43 per cent. Wages, salaries, and prices all remained comparatively stable, or in any case underwent no comparable increase. Accordingly, costs fell and with prices the same, profits increased. These profits sustained the spending of the well-to-do, and they also nourished at least some of the expectations behind the stock market boom. Most of all they encouraged a very high level of capital investment. During the twenties, the production of capital goods increased at an average annual rate of 6.4 per cent a year; non-durable consumers' good, a category which includes such objects of mass consumption as food and clothing, increased at a rate of only 2.8 per cent. (The rate of increase for durable consumers' goods such as cars, dwellings, home furnishings, and the like, much of it representing expenditures of the well-off to well-to-do, was 5.9 per cent.) A large and increasing investment in capital goods was, in other words, a principal device by which the profits were being spent. It follows that anything that interrupted the investment outlays — anything, indeed, which kept them from showing the necessary rate of increase — could cause trouble. When this occurred, compensation through an increase in consumer spending could not automatically be expected. The effect, therefore, of insufficient investment — investment that failed to keep pace with the steady increase in profits — could be falling total demand reflected in turn in falling orders and output. Again there is no final proof of this point, for unfortunately we do not know how rapidly investment had to grow to keep abreast of the current increase in profits.[1] However, the explanation is broadly consistent with the facts.

There are other possible explanations of the downturn. Back of the insufficient advance in investment may have been the high interest rates. Perhaps, although less probably, trouble was transmitted to the economy as a whole from some weak sector like agriculture. Further explanations could be offered. But one thing about this experience is clear. Until well along in the autumn of 1929 the downturn was limited. The recession in business activity was modest and underemployment relatively slight. Up to November it was possible to argue that not

much of anything had happened. On other occasions, as noted — in 1924 and 1927 and of late in 1949 — the economy has undergone similar recession. But, unlike these other occasions, in 1929 the recession continued and continued and got violently worse. This is the unique feature of the 1929 experience. This is what we need really to understand.

There seems little question that in 1929, modifying a famous cliché, the economy was fundamentally unsound. This is a circumstance of first-rate importance. Many things were wrong, but five weaknesses seem to have had an especially intimate bearing on the ensuing disaster. They are:

1) The bad distribution of income. In 1929 the rich were indubitably rich. The figures are not entirely satisfactory, but it seems certain that the 5 per cent of the population with the highest incomes in that year received approximately one third of all personal income. The proportion of personal income received in the form of interest, dividends, and rent — the income, broadly speaking, of the well-to-do —was about twice as great as in the years following the Second World War.

This highly unequal income distribution meant that the economy was dependent on a high level of investment or a high level of luxury consumer spending or both. The rich cannot buy great quantities of bread. If they are to dispose of what they receive it must be on luxuries or by way of investment in new plants and new projects. Both investment and luxury spending are subject, inevitably, to more erratic influences and to wider fluctuations than the bread and rent outlays of the $25-a-week workman. This high-bracket spending and investment was especially susceptible, one may assume, to the crushing news from the

[1] Perhaps I may be permitted to enlarge on this in slightly more technical terms. The interruption could as well have been caused by an insufficient rate of increase in consumer spending by a failure in the greater rate of increase of capital goods spending. Under-consumption and under-investment are the same side of the same coin. And some force is added to this explanation by the fact that spending for one important consumers' durable, namely houses, had been declining for several years and suffered a further substantial drop in 1929. However, the investment function we still suppose to be less stable than the consumption function, even though we are less assured of the stability of the latter than we used to be. And in the present case it seems wise to attach causal significance to the part of the spending which had to maintain the largest rate of increase if total spending were to be uninterrupted. The need to maintain a specific rate of increase in investment outlay is insufficiently emphasized by Mr. Thomas Wilson in his book which I have so frequently cited and to which students of the period are indebted.

stock market in October of 1929.

2) The bad corporate structure. In November 1929, a few weeks after the crash, the Harvard Economic Society gave as a principal reason why a depression need not be feared its reasoned judgment that "business in most lines has been conducted with prudence and conservatism." The fact was that American enterprise in the twenties had opened its hospitable arms to an exceptional number of promoters, grafters, swindlers, impostors, and frauds. This, in the long history of such activities, was a kind of flood tide of corporate larceny.

The most important corporate weakness was inherent in the vast new structure of holding companies and investment trusts. The holding companies controlled large segments of the utility, railroad, and entertainment business. Here, as with the investment trusts, was the constant danger of devastation by reverse leverage. In particular, dividends from the operating companies paid the interest on the bonds of upstream holding companies. The interruption of the dividend meant default on the bonds, bankruptcy, and the collapse of the structure. Under these circumstances, the temptation to curtail investment in operating plant in order to continue dividends was obviously strong. This added to deflationary pressures. The latter, in turn, curtailed earnings and helped bring down the corporate pyramids. When this happened, even more retrenchment was inevitable. Income was earmarked for debt repayment. Borrowing for new investment became impossible. It would be hard to imagine a corporate system better designed to continue and accentuate a deflationary spiral.

3) The bad banking structure. Since the early thirties, a generation of Americans has been told, sometimes with amusement, sometimes with indignation, often with outrage, of the banking practices of the late twenties. In fact, many of these practices were made ludicrous only by the depression. Loans which would have been perfectly good were made perfectly foolish by the collapse of the borrower's prices or the markets for his goods or the value of the collateral he had posted. The most responsible bankers — those who saw that their debtors were victims of circumstances far beyond their control and sought to help — were often made to look the worst. The bankers yielded, as did others, to the blithe, optimistic, and immoral mood of times but probably not more so. A depression such as that of 1929–32, were it to begin as this is written, would also be damaging to many currently impeccable banking reputations.

However, although the bankers were not unusually foolish in 1929, the banking structure was inherently weak. The weakness was implicit in the large numbers of independent units. When one bank failed, the assets of others were frozen while depositors elsewhere had a pregnant warning to go and ask for their money. Thus one failure led to other failures, and these spread with a domino effect. Even in the best of times local misfortune or isolated mismanagement could start such a chain reaction. (In the first six months of 1929, 346 banks failed in various parts of the country with aggregate deposits of nearly $115 million.) When income, employment, and values fell as the result of a depression bank failures could quickly become epidemic. This happened after 1929. Again it would be hard to imagine a better arrangement for magnifying the effects of fear. The weak destroyed not only the other weak, but weakened the strong. People everywhere, rich and poor, were made aware of the disaster by the persuasive intelligence that their savings had been destroyed.

Needless to say, such a banking system, once in the convulsions of failure, had a uniquely repressive effect on the spending of its depositors and the investment of its clients.

4) The dubious state of the foreign balance. This is a familiar story. During the First World War, the United States became a creditor on international account. In the decade following, the surplus of exports over imports which once had paid the interest and principal on loans from Europe continued. The high tariffs, which restricted imports and helped to create this surplus of exports remained. However, history and traditional trading habits also accounted for the persistence of the favorable balance, so called.

Before, payments on interest and principal had in effect been deducted from the trade balance. Now that the United States was a creditor, they were added to this balance. The latter, it should be said, was not huge. In only one year (1928) did the excess of exports over imports come to as much as a billion dollars; in 1923 and 1926 it was only about $375,000,000. However, large or small, this difference had to be covered. Other countries which were buying more than they sold, and had debt payments to make in addition, had somehow to find the means for making up the deficit in their transactions with the United States.

During most of the twenties the difference was covered by cash — i.e., gold payments to the United States — and by new private loans by the United States to other countries. Most of the loans were to governments — national, state, or municipal bodies — and a large proportion

were to Germany and Central and South America. The underwriters' margins in handling these loans were generous; the public took them up with enthusiasm; competition for the business was keen. If unfortunately corruption and bribery were required as competitive instruments, these were used. In late 1927 Juan Leguia, the son of the President of Peru, was paid $450,000 by J. and W. Seligman and Company and the National City Company (the security affiliate of the National City Bank) for his services in connection with a $50,000,000 loan which these houses marketed for Peru. Juan's services, according to later testimony, were of a rather negative sort. He was paid for not blocking the deal. The Chase extended President Machado of Cuba, a dictator with a marked predisposition toward murder, a generous personal line of credit which at one time reached $200,000. Machado's son-in-law was employed by the Chase. The bank did a large business in Cuban bonds. In contemplating these loans, there was a tendency to pass quickly over anything that might appear to the disadvantage of the creditor. Mr. Victor Schoepperle, a vice-president of the National City Company with the responsibility for Latin American loans, made the following appraisal of Peru as a credit prospect:

Peru: Bad debt record, adverse moral and political risk, bad internal debt situation, trade situation about as satisfactory as that of Chile in the past three years. Natural resources more varied. On economic showing Peru should go ahead rapidly in the next 10 years.

On such showing the National City Company floated a $15,000,000 loan for Peru, followed a few months later by a $50,000,000 loan, and some ten months thereafter by a $25,000,000 issue. (Peru did prove a highly adverse political risk. President Leguia, who negotiated the loans, was thrown violently out of office, and the loans went into default.)

In all respects these operations were as much a part of the New Era as Shenandoah and Blue Ridge. They were also just as fragile, and once the illusions of the New Era were dissipated they came as abruptly to an end. This, in turn, forced a fundamental revision in the foreign economic position of the United States. Countries could not cover their adverse trade balance with the United States with increased payments of gold, at least not for long. This meant that they had either to increase their exports to the United States or reduce their imports or default on their past loans. President Hoover and the Congress moved promptly to eliminate the first possibility — that the accounts would be balanced by larger imports — by sharply increasing the tariff. Accordingly, debts, including war debts, went into default and there was a precipitate fall in American exports. The reduction was not vast in relation to total output of the American economy, but it contributed to the general distress and was especially hard on farmers.

5) The poor state of economic intelligence. To regard the people of any time as particularly obtuse seems vaguely improper, and it also establishes a precedent which members of this generation might regret. Yet it seems certain that the economists and those who offered economic counsel in the late twenties and early thirties were almost uniquely perverse. In the months and years following the stock market crash, the burden of reputable economic advice was invariably on the side of measures that would make things worse. In November

of 1929, Mr. Hoover announced a cut in taxes; in the great no-business conferences that followed he asked business firms to keep up their capital investment and to maintain wages. Both of these measures were on the side of increasing spendable income, though unfortunately they were largely without effect. The tax reductions were negligible except in the higher income brackets; businessmen who promised to maintain investment and wages, in accordance with a well-understood convention, considered the promise binding only for the period within which it was not financially disadvantageous to do so. As a result investment outlays and wages were not reduced until circumstances would in any case have brought their reduction.

Still, the effort was in the right direction. Thereafter policy was almost entirely on the side of making things worse. Asked how the government could best advance recovery, the sound and responsible adviser urged that the budget be balanced. Both parties agreed on this. For Republicans the balanced budget was, as ever, high doctrine. But the Democratic Party platform of 1932, with an explicitness which politicians rarely advise, also called for a "federal budget annually balanced on the basis of accurate executive estimates within revenues . . ."

A commitment to a balanced budget is always comprehensive. It then meant there could be no increase in government outlays to expand purchasing power and relieve distress. It meant there could be no further tax reduction. But taken literally it meant much more. From 1930 on the budget was far out of balance, and balance, therefore, meant an increase in taxes, a reduction in spending, or both. The Democratic platform in 1932 called for an "immediate and drastic reduction

94 THE GREAT DEPRESSION

of governmental expenditures" to accomplish at least a 25 per cent decrease in the cost of government.

The balanced budget was not a subject of thought. Nor was it, as often asserted, precisely a matter of faith. Rather it was a formula. For centuries avoidance of borrowing had protected people from slovenly or reckless public housekeeping. Slovenly or reckless keepers of the public purse had often composed complicated arguments to show why balance of income and outlay was not a mark of virtue. Experience had shown that however convenient this belief might seem in the short run, discomfort or disaster followed in the long run. Those simple precepts of a simple world did not hold amid the growing complexities of the early thirties. Mass unemployment in particular had altered the rules. Events had played a very bad trick on people, but almost no one tried to think out the problem anew.

The balanced budget was not the only strait jacket on policy. There was also the bogey of "going off" the gold standard and, most surprisingly, of risking inflation. Until 1932 the United States added formidably to its gold reserves, and instead of inflation the country was experiencing the most violent deflation in the nation's history. Yet every sober adviser saw dangers here, including the danger of runaway price increases. Americans, though in years now well in the past, had shown a penchant for tinkering with the money supply and enjoying the brief but heady joys of a boom in prices. In 1931 or 1932, the danger or even the feasibility of such a boom was nil. The advisers and counselors were not, however, analyzing the danger or even the possibility. They were serving only as the custodians of bad memories.

The fear of inflation reinforced the demand for the balanced budget. It also limited efforts to make interest rates low, credit plentiful (or at least redundant) and borrowing as easy as possible under the circumstances. Devaluation of the dollar was, of course, flatly ruled out. This directly violated the gold standard rules. At best, in such depression times, monetary policy is a feeble reed on which to lean. The current economic clichés did not allow even the use of that frail weapon. And again, these attitudes were above party. Though himself singularly open-minded, Roosevelt was careful not to offend or disturb his followers. In a speech in Brooklyn toward the close of the 1932 campaign, he said:

The Democratic platform specifically declares, "We advocate a sound currency to be preserved at all hazards." That is plain English. In discussing this platform on July 30, I said, "Sound money is an international necessity, not a domestic consideration for one nation alone." Far up in the Northwest, at Butte, I repeated the pledge . . . In Seattle I reaffirmed my attitude . . .

The following February, Mr. Hoover set forth his view, as often before, in a famous letter to the President-elect:

It would steady the country greatly if there could be prompt assurance that there will be no tampering or inflation of the currency; that the budget will be unquestionably balanced even if further taxation is necessary; that the Government credit will be maintained by refusal to exhaust it in the issue of securities.

The rejection of both fiscal (tax and expenditure) and monetary policy amounted precisely to a rejection of all affirmative government economic policy. The economic advisers of the day had both the unanimity and the authority to force the leaders of both parties to disavow all the available steps to check deflation and depression. In its own way this was a marked achievement — a triumph of dogma over thought. The consequences were profound.

It is in light of the above weaknesses of the economy that the role of the stock market crash in the great tragedy of the thirties must be seen. The years of self-depreciation by Wall Street to the contrary, the role is one of respectable importance. The collapse in securities values affected in the first instance the wealthy and the well-to-do. But we see that in the world of 1929 this was a vital group. The members disposed of a large proportion of the consumer income; they were the source of a lion's share of personal saving and investment. Anything that struck at the spending or investment by this group would of necessity have broad effects on expenditure and income in the economy at large. Precisely such a blow was struck by the stock market crash. In addition, the crash promptly removed from the economy the support that it had been deriving from the spending of stock market gains.

The stock market crash was also an exceptionally effective way of exploiting the weaknesses of the corporate structure. Operating companies at the end of the holding-company chain were forced by the crash to retrench. The subsequent collapse of these systems and also of the investment trusts effectively destroyed both the ability to borrow and the willingness to lend for investment. What have long looked like purely fiduciary effects were, in fact, quickly translated into declining orders and increasing unemployment.

The crash was also effective in bringing to an end the foreign lending by which the international accounts had been balanced. Now the accounts had, in the main, to be balanced by reduced exports. This put prompt and heavy pressure on export markets for wheat, cotton, and tobacco. Perhaps the foreign loans had only delayed an adjustment in the balance which had one day to come. The stock market crash served nonetheless to precipitate the adjustment with great suddenness at a most unpropitious time. The instinct of farmers who traced their troubles to the stock market was not totally misguided.

Finally, when the misfortune had struck, the attitudes of the time kept anything from being done about it. This, perhaps, was the most disconcerting feature of all. Some people were hungry in 1930 and 1931 and 1932. Others were tortured by the fear that they might go hungry. Yet others suffered the agony of the descent from the honor and respectability that goes with income into poverty. And still others feared that they would be next. Meanwhile everyone suffered from a sense of utter hopelessness. Nothing, it seemed, could be done. And given the ideas which controlled policy, nothing could be done.

Had the economy been fundamentally sound in 1929 the effect of the great stock market crash might have been small. Alternatively, the shock to confidence and the loss of spending by those who were caught in the market might soon have worn off. But business in 1929 was not sound; on the contrary it was exceedingly fragile. It was vulnerable to the kind of blow it received from Wall Street. Those who have emphasized this vulnerability are obviously on strong ground. Yet when a greenhouse succumbs to a hailstorm something more than a purely passive role is normally attributed to the storm. One must accord similar significance to the typhoon which blew out of lower Manhattan in October 1929.

John Chamberlain: INDUSTRIAL INVENTION AND PROGRESS: THE QUALITATIVE VIGOR OF BUSINESS IN THE THIRTIES

John Chamberlain, a noted journalist and commentator on the economic and political scene, and author of articles appearing in such publications as Fortune *and the* Wall Street Journal, *published in 1963* The Enterprising Americans, *from which the following selection is taken. As the reader will observe, his discussion of the causes of stagnation in the 1930's derives directly from the Schumpeterian outlook. Chamberlain, however, writing after the tremendous postwar expansion of the American economy, avoids Schumpeter's conclusion that the New Deal reforms implied a gradual stultification of the capitalist system. Instead, he maintains that technological advances continuing despite the failure of many New Deal reforms made it possible for the economy to rebound under the impact of mobilization.*

IN THE first hundred days of the New Deal there came a new wave of optimism. In many ways it seemed to be justified. President Roosevelt was magnificently right in seeing that confidence was the key to the situation, and his own courage and jaunty optimism — "there is nothing to fear but fear itself" — did much to break the mood of despair and national paralysis. But the baffling question, to which historians have paid all too little attention, is why business confidence was never fully restored, and why the great depression dragged on for six more painful years. In 1933, when F.D.R. gave his first fireside chat, there were some thirteen million unemployed in the U.S. As late as 1939 there were still nine million unemployed men and women, and on the record it was not Doctor New Deal but Doctor Win the War who, in Roosevelt's phrase, finally put the country back to work.

The expansion of this failure of the New Deal to accomplish its primary mission lies partly in Roosevelt's inability to decide for himself just what he was putting his confidence in. His far-reaching decision to follow Britain off gold was reflationary in purpose, but his subsequent failure to restore full redeemability of the currency, once the metal had been repriced, deprived the U.S. and the world of a needed monetary discipline. Many of his business reforms — notably his insistence on "truth in securities" and the setting up of the SEC — were long overdue; others were frankly punitive. With reason, businessmen came to ask themselves whether Roosevelt really understood a system where the hope of profit sparks expansion and investment. Or did he believe simply in centralizing decision and authority in boards and "planners" along the Potomac?

The first important domestic creation of the New Deal, the NRA, was a total abnegation of the competitive market economy. A peacetime adaptation of Bernard Baruch's old War Industries Board of World War I days, the NRA appealed to some businessmen who preferred the cartel system of Europe to doing business competitively under the

From John Chamberlain, *The Enterprising Americans: A Business History of the United States* (New York: Harper Colophon Books, 1963), pp. 230–42. Reprinted by permission of the author.

Sherman Act. Under General Hugh (Iron Pants) Johnson the new experiment made a tremendous noise. But with its price-fixing and market-allocating codes the NRA was a denial of the free system, and before it was thrown out by the Supreme Court its critics were referring to it as "Chamber of Commerce Fascism." Its inherent contradictions were later freely admitted by Administration intellectuals themselves when in Roosevelt's second term they set up the Temporary National Economic Committee to restore competitive pricing, while at the same time embracing the doctrine of Keynesian spending to restore purchasing power.

The difficulty with this new palliative was that its success depended uniquely on the restoration of profitability in the system. The Keynesians remembered that their master had argued against wage cuts; labor, he said, is seldom in a mood to take a cut-back. But he had certainly not called for money wage *increases* in a time of deflation when real wages were going up every time a retail price fell. To restore both profitability and purchasing power, the Keynesian formula called for a turn-about in prices through the government spending as existing wage rates were maintained. Perversely, however, the American disciples of Keynes paid no heed to the role which profitability via rising prices pays in luring investment money from hiding. They overlooked the fact that money wage rates in manufacturing advanced some 43 per cent between 1933 and 1939 and *real* wages by an extraordinary 34 per cent, which, on Keynes's own theory, was detrimental to curing the surplus of labor. Some of this rise was no doubt to be expected in a period of partial recovery, but much of it flowed out of government-blessed wage boosts from an unprece-

dented surge of union organization. When NRA was buried, the provisions of its Section 7a were incorporated into the lopsided Wagner Act, which gave John L. Lewis, Walter Reuther, and others a free hunting license to push industrial unionism in the basic mass-production industries. In a free system labor has the incontestable right to organize and to bargain collectively; and it had exercised this right long before the New Deal. But the very rapidity of the spread of unionism in the thirties, beyond pushing up costs, was scarcely conducive to restoring business confidence. And the tactics of the sitdown strike, however effective in bringing companies like General Motors to heel, did nothing to encourage private investment in new industrial plant.

The pay-off story, indeed, is suggested by the figures for industrial profits and private investment — the key to industrial advance in a capitalist system. From their inflated peak of $8.3 billion in 1929, corporate profits after taxes plunged to minus $3.4 billion in 1932, recovered to $4.7 billion in 1937, and then collapsed again in 1938. Domestic investment followed the same pattern, falling from $16 billion in 1929 to a bare $900 million in 1932, rising to an $11.7-billion temporary peak in 1937, and then dropping back to $6.7 billion in the 1938 slide. Under such circumstances it is little wonder that the economy failed to pick up the huge pools of unemployed left by the crash and open new job opportunities for the growing labor force. To uncertainties at home must be added the facts that despite Cordell Hull's drive for a reciprocal lowering of tariffs the Roosevelt regime remained highly nationalistic in its orientation, but autarkic governments were everywhere sprouting in Europe, and that expanding world trade, based on freely convertible currencies, was hardly compatible with European and Asiatic preparations for coming military showdowns. Indeed, it was not until war orders from Europe broke the pattern that the famous Keynesian "multiplier" took hold.

Yet the magnitude of the response of U.S. business to the war is in itself refutation of the thesis that in the thirties businessmen simply sat on their hands and the economy reached "maturity." The really surprising thing about the decade, in fact, is that while investment was quantitatively lower than needed to restore full employment, it was *qualitatively* impressive. While many men were lamenting the disappearance of the old western frontier and the lack of a new "ladder" industry such as automobiles, technological advance continued without abatement, and the scientific revolution took hold. In time this revolution, gathering a momentum of its own, would produce frontier after frontier and ladder after ladder at a pace almost too dizzy to follow.

The big sleeper of the thirties was the chemical industry, which began its march toward making "anything out of anything." To use the term "sleeper" for the chemical thirties is to speak relatively, of course, for important companies had already begun to wheel themselves into place as far back as 1920. The first forward step came during World War I, when the British blockade of the central European powers cut America off from all sorts of German dyes, drugs, and synthetics. In early 1916, Lammot du Pont, whose M.I.T. degree was in mechanical engineering, took charge of a new "miscellaneous" department of his company that was destined to manufacture dyes, paints, lacquers, pyralin, and plastics. Included in the "miscellany" was synthetic indigo, for which $600,000 in pow-

der profits was set aside to build a plant. Allied Chemical moved out from bulk inorganics into coke byproducts and dyestuffs in addition to the older acids and alkalies; Union Carbide, whose newest division was busy with automobile antifreeze as early as 1920, took the leadership in the development of petrochemicals, a division of organic chemistry that is based on a straight-line chain of carbon atoms instead of the famous six-carbon benzene ring from which coal-tar products are derived.

The "Big Three" of du Pont, Allied Chemical, and Union Carbide all had to meet terrific development expenses throughout the twenties, but forged steadily ahead. Du Pont, an early rayon producer, took a pioneer position as a supplier of synthetic and semi-synthetic materials for both the textile and the container and wrapper industries. Because of its work in rayon the company had formed a tie with the French Comptoir de Textiles Artificiels, which had financed a Swiss-born French chemist, Jacques Edwin Brandenberger, in the development of cellophane. In 1926 two du Pont chemists, William Hale Charch and Karl Edwin Prindle, found a way to waterproof cellophane — and with the new waterproofed magical wrapper the company really went to town. ("You're the tops, you're cellophane," sang Cole Porter.) By 1933 the demand for cellophane was so heavy that du Pont, not wishing to tie up too much capital in any single product, licensed the Sylvania Industrial Corp. to produce the stuff.

The du Pont triumph in waterproofed cellophane was merely one of a number of accomplishments that took the company pretty much out of the munitions business long before Senator Gerald Nye and his war-profits investigating committee of the thirties traduced the big

Wilmington concern as a "merchant of death." Its tie with General Motors strengthened this tendency, providing an additional outlet and a stimulus for its new chemical skills. Early in the twenties a General Motors research team headed by Thomas Midgley and Charles Kettering, neither of whom was a chemist, discovered that tetraethyl lead would eliminate the "knock" from gasoline. The practical process of safely distilling tetraethyl lead in commercial quantities was developed by a Clark University professor, Dr. Charles A. Kraus, and his assistant, Dr. Conrad C. Callis, for the Standard Oil Co. of New Jersey, which shortly combined with General Motors to set up a joint subsidiary, the Ethyl Gasoline Corp. Lacking facilities to make its own tetraethyl lead in quantity, the Ethyl company turned to the du Ponts, who proceeded to supply it in large and profitable amounts. And in the thirties a du Pont-G.M. subsidiary provided dichlorodifluoromethane (Freon), another Midgley-Kettering product, for the refrigerant that went into G.M.'s Frigidaires.

Success with such items as rayon and waterproofed cellophane spurred the du Ponts to the most important decision of their latter-day existence as a company, which was to enter the field of pure — or fundamental — research. To head the new program, Dr. Wallace H. Carothers was plucked in 1928 from the faculty of Harvard University, where he had already distinguished himself with his studies of the structure of substances of high molecular weight. Once ensconced in his du Pont laboratory, where he had an annual fund of $250,000 to play with, Dr. Carothers began working on the synthesis of the long-chain— or polymerizing — molecules that form the basic building blocks of living tissue. In April of 1930, when people everywhere were despairing of the ability of private enterprise to turn up new and profitable lines, Dr. Carothers and his crew of assistants watched as the first "thread" of a new long-chain substance, silk-like and strong, was drawn out of a laboratory still. Four years later Carothers and his team had succeeded in getting a synthetic filament that was proof against attack by heat, solvents, and water. And four years after this, in 1938, nylon was at last ready to go in a pilot plant. Altogether, the du Ponts spent $27 million — $6 million for research, $21 million for plant — to put nylon on the market. The first pair of nylon stockings was offered for sale in May of 1940 — and by 1941 du Pont operating capacity for nylon was more than two million miles of yarn a day. Some 400 textile mills, cut off from their sources of raw silk for stockings by the attack on Pearl Harbor, grabbed for the stuff. Nylon also went into toothbrush bristles, tennis racquets, fishing rods, and self-lubricating bearings.

Other du Pont triumphs of the thirties include Lucite, synthesized musk oil (a basis for fine perfumes), and the merchandising of neoprene, the basis for a synthetic rubber. Meanwhile Union Carbide, which had bought the Bakelite Co., the earliest hard-plastic manufacturer in the country, for $11 million in stock, was also expanding its oxygen and acetylene plants, and proliferating with chemicals and alloys. Behind Allied Chemical & Dye and Union Carbide & Carbon there were a profusion of lesser companies: Dow Chemical, a bulk chlorine producer, which perfected styrene for synthetic rubber; American Cyanamid, the first developer of a nitrogen-fixation process; Monsanto, which moved by way of coal-tar-based organics into petrochemicals and plastics; and the oil companies, which developed the Houdry catalytic-cracking process. In addition, there were fertilizer companies which possessed the industrial skills that would erupt in a vast array of fungicides, herbicides, soil conditioners, defoliants, and insecticides after World War II. In 1934 agricultural-chemical production amounted to 100 million pounds; after the war the poundage would soar to a yearly two billion.

While chemistry was leaping out of the test tubes of the thirties, industrial physics was hardly quiescent, and there were also developments on that strange frontier where physics and chemistry meet. Rumors of an atom-smashing cyclotron came from the University of California laboratory of Dr. Ernest O. Lawrence, and this suggested new sources of industrial power. General Electric, on the advice of Dr. Arthur H. Compton, went into fluorescent lighting; Carrier went ahead with air conditioning. Electronics hit a commercial plateau period in the thirties as radio continued to prosper; but Vladimir Zworykin of R.C.A. worked throughout the decade to clarify the television image projected by his iconoscope, and Philo Farnsworth, a free lance, developed independent television patents. The FCC, which professed to have protective feelings about the average citizen's investment in his radio receiving set, dawdled over granting a commercial television license until 1940 — so the first leap forward in putting television sets into homes was postponed by government fiat. But in Britain, where there were fewer shackles in such matters, the first electronic television system was set up in 1936.

Standing at the crossroads where optics and chemistry come together, the Eastman Kodak Co. worked all through the twenties and early thirties on the problem of making color photography a commercial proposition. The first processes all had flaws, and it remained for two concert musicians, Leo Godowsky and Leopold Mannes, who had made photography a hobby, to come up with a three-color dye-coupling developing process and a film that was no more complicated to use than the traditional black-and-white. Invited to join the Kodak organization at a good salary-cum-patent-royalty figure, Mannes and Godowsky perfected the color film that was finally put on the market by Eastman under the name of Kodachrome in 1935. Eastman also kept a close watch on the development of a synthetic light-polarizing material, obtaining the rights to the use of Edwin H. Land's invention as it related to photographic filters. The sagacious Land, a young Harvard student when he started work on his polarizer, also licensed American Optical and Bausch & Lomb to use his patents in making sunglasses and optical instruments and went on to form the Polaroid Corp. for himself.

Despite the depression in heavy industries in the thirties, Alcoa made the continuous casting of aluminum standard practice. The hot continuous rolling of wide-strip steel was pioneered by the American Rolling Mill Co.'s John B. Tytus, who had first installed his cylinders at an Ashland, Kentucky, subsidiary of Armco as early as 1923. The son of a paper manufacturer, Tytus had watched huge rolls of paper emerging in a long strip from the mills of his father. In a roughly analogous way he adapted this to the making of steel sheet. Tytus' patents gave Armco a long headstart on the rest of the steel community, but in the thirties other companies, while honoring Armco's patents, began to catch up. National Steel, a relatively small company, was the first to introduce the Steckel mill, a system for rolling extra-thin steel sheets. Under tough Ernest Weir, National Steel boldly moved into the Detroit area, making handsome profits while older-line companies were floundering, and introduced new and needed competition into the entire industry.

Harold Ickes's public-works program helped shore up a depressed market for heavy structural steel. But as the thirties progressed, private orders also started to flush the mills into larger activity. Kettering of General Motors, whose hobby was a diesel yacht, had perfected a diesel-electric engine that could be used also to pull railroad cars — and just as the railroad business seemed to be on the verge of floundering because of high costs, it was suddenly discovered that high-speed diesel-drawn trains could make money. Western roads such as the Burlington, the Union Pacific, and the Santa Fe started diesel-drawn streamlined service, and soon the eastern roads were following suit with both diesel and electric streamliners. Within a few short years, with 48,000 miles of high-speed tracks available in the U.S., the rolling stock of the roads had taken on a modern appearance.

Next to chemistry, it was the aviation business that really marked the decade of the thirties for its own. Although the Wright brothers had flown as early as 1903, which was the same year in which the Ford Motor Co. got its start, the airplane had taken much longer than the automobile to realize its potential. The U.S. Army got interested in the airplane around 1908, but neither the military strategists nor the tacticians seemed to know what the plane might be used for in wartime. In 1917 the automobile men, notably Howard Coffin of Hudson, John N. Willys, Ford, and Henry Leland, made Liberty engines for aircraft. American planes, however, were not manufac-

tured in time to affect the issue over the battle lines in France.

Thus it happened that American aces like Eddie Rickenbacker flew British and French planes over the World War I trenches. They returned to the U.S. hoping to make a true business out of air transport. In 1923, Juan Terry Trippe, just a year after his belated graduation from Yale, quit his job as a bond salesman and, with his friend John Hambleton, bid a total of $4,500 for nine Navy flying boats that were about to be junked. Trading off some of these planes for better models, Trippe and Hambleton tried running a plane taxi service around New York, only to find themselves going broke. In 1925, however, the Kelly Air Mail Act authorized the Post Office Department to sign contracts with private companies for carrying mail at rates running up to $3 a pound, which made commercial flying a real possibility. Helped by Cornelius Vanderbilt Whitney and William H. Vanderbilt, Trippe and Hambleton scraped up enough cash to start Eastern Air Transport. This company joined forces with Colonial Airways to become Colonial Air Transport, which started to carry New York to Boston mail. At just about the same time Charles Lindbergh, then an Army reserve flyer, began carrying the mail for the Robertson Aircraft Corp. on the St. Louis-Chicago run.

Between them, as it turned out, Trippe and Lindbergh did more than any other two individuals to set the U.S. on the road to the development of air transport. Visiting Havana in 1927, Trippe sewed up an exclusive landing permit from President Machado of Cuba, which gave him control of the bottleneck to the Caribbean region and so made Pan American Airways a possibility. And in that same year Lindberg made his solo flight across the Atlantic, hitting Le

Bourget field near Paris right on the nose. Lindbergh's flight sparked increasing interest in Wall Street, as evidenced by the growth of holding companies like North American Aviation Inc. It also led to the formation of domestic carriers like United Air Lines and Eastern (originally called Pitcairn after its founder). Meanwhile, T.W.A. developed as a midcontinental carrier, and Cyrus Rowlett — or "C.R." — Smith began to build American Airlines into a transcontinental company. Other big domestic airlines were built in the thirties, and scores of "feeders" were consolidated with them.

Looking beyond the continental limits of the U.S., Trippe's Pan American Airways had things pretty much to itself at the start. Running his own private diplomatic service, Trippe negotiated flight-landing agreements with strategic countries on both the west and east coasts of South America. When mollifying deals were necessary, he shared arrangements with local airlines (often run by Germans) as well as with Grace steamship interests. But always he pushed the claims of Pan American Airways as a "chosen instrument," able to deliver service that lesser aspirants could not guarantee to postmaster generals. With a shrewd sense of public relations as well as of flying skills, he employed Lindbergh to pioneer some of his first Caribbean routes. Despite some stockholder recalcitrance, he pushed Pan American across the Pacific in the mid-thirties, establishing airports on lonely islands that turned out to have inestimable military value when war came.

Pan American service to the Philippines and Macao and Hong Kong off the coast of China had been reduced pretty much to routine operations well before the commercial conquest of the Atlantic, which was held up until 1939 because of disagreements between London and Washington over the right to airport facilities spotted along the British approaches to the North American continent. Eventually the diplomatic snarls were straightened out, and Pan Am spanned the Atlantic just in time to set a pattern of operations for the thousands of military transport planes that would shortly be carrying soldiers and civilian V.I.P.'s to London and Lisbon on the edge of the Nazis' Fortress Europa.

The development of aviation in the thirties did more than open the vital air routes. To produce planes for Pan American and the domestic big four, airframe companies began to dot the U.S., including Martin at Baltimore, Boeing at Seattle, Douglas at Santa Monica, all of which created a vast new demand for the Mellons' aluminum. Donald Douglas' famous DC-3 first took to the air in 1936. With its retractable landing gear, its variable-pitch propeller, and its 180-mile-an-hour cruising speed, the DC-3 was among the first planes to make passengers feel like something more than unprofitable additions to baggage, and later it turned into the great and beloved workhorse of World War II. Meanwhile huge Sikorsky, Martin, and Boeing clippers came to discharge Pan American passengers, mail, and cargo at the ends of the earth in Auckland, New Zealand, and later in the Congo. Into these planes went myriad instruments produced by old and new companies such as Sperry Gyroscope and Collins Radio. And Curtiss-Wright and United Aircraft turned out radial motors of ever increasing horsepower until the piston engine itself began to give place to the jet.

This whole complex of engineering skills helped beleaguered Britain in 1939 and likewise helped produce the "miracle" of production after Pearl Harbor.

When President Roosevelt in a famous defense message called for 20,000 planes, the skeptics laughed. But in the course of the war an industry that, in the preceding twenty years, had made fewer than 30,000 planes was able to turn out some 300,000 with an assist from Detroit. The ability of the economy to make air power a reality was only one manifestation of its latent strength. Once firm war orders were placed, military paraphernalia of all types poured off the production lines. In 1918 General von Hindenburg in defeat had remarked sadly of the U.S. industrial effort under Baruch's War Industries Board: "Those men understood war." In World War II this accolade was doubly applicable. The automobile industry alone produced 200,000 tanks and gun carriages, 450,000 aircraft engines, 2,300,000 machine guns, and some 2,600,000 Army trucks, while continuing with its left hand to turn out the spare parts to keep some 26 million cars on the roads.

Thus the Great Depression ended on a new affirmation of industrial power, and under the impact of mobilization unemployment vanished as if by sleight of hand. Political veterans who remember the struggles of the thirties are quick to argue, of course, that the rapid achievement of full and overfull employment proves that they were right all along in their assertion that the private economy had become hopelessly static and could only be revitalized by vast dosages of government spending and government "investment." Yet had the economy of the thirties been really "mature" it would simply not have been able to produce a new type of goods when the war button was pressed. Moreover, it should be observed that war spending involved a huge social as well as financial cost. For to lessen the worst ravages of inflation the U.S. had to impose all manner of controls and, in fact, adopted an authoritarian economic system. With its ration cards and multiplying directives from Washington agencies, such a system would not be accepted for peacetime use in a free society.

The Keynesian analysis, when properly understood and qualified, adds a useful dimension to economic discourse. But in its more radical interpretation it obscures the problem of combining general stability with the flexibility and decentralization of the market economy. The reconciliation of large defense spending, made necessary by the Russian danger, with limited constitutional government and with voluntary economic enterprise became, as we shall see, a challenge of the fifties. It is a challenge that is still with us, and it will hardly lessen as we reach out to shoot the moon.

Robert A. Gordon: EXHAUSTION OF INVESTMENT OPPORTUNITIES

Robert A. Gordon, Professor of Economics at the University of California since 1938, gives us in the following selection perhaps the most useful and stimulating interpretation of the Great Depression yet worked out by an economist. For a longer and more detailed version of this appraisal, see his "Cyclical Experience in the Interwar Period: The Investment Boom of the 'Twenties," in Conference on Business Cycles *(New York: National Bureau of Economic Research, 1951), pp. 163–215.*

BUSINESS recovered rapidly from the depression of 1921, and by 1923 total output substantially exceeded the peak reached in 1919–1920. From 1923 through 1929, business remained at a high level and tended to increase still further, with minor interruptions in 1924 and 1927. The period culminated with a particularly large increase in industrial output and total GNP in 1929.

* * *

The outstanding fact about the movement of total capital formation in this decade is the high level reached by 1923 and the maintenance of this level for seven years. We have here a prolonged period of high-level investment in producers' durable goods and construction. Inventory accumulation and foreign investment did not play the same important role that they did in 1919–1920. For the period 1923–1929 as a whole, total capital formation averaged about 19.5 billion dollars (in 1929 prices), compared to 11.7 billions in the prewar decade 1904–1913. It is significant that both producers' and consumers' durables formed a larger fraction of the GNP during the 1920's than during any period before World War I.

We thus have a picture of a prolonged

investment boom, which supported a steady expansion in incomes and consumers' demand and at the same time provided the enlarged capacity necessary to meet the rising demand for goods and services. An understanding of the business-cycle history of the 1920's and 1930's lies very largely, though not entirely, in the causes and nature of this investment boom.

* * *

The main underlying factors responsible for the high level of investment in the 1920's were: (1) pent-up demands for plant and equipment created by the war (2) the direct and indirect effects of the automobile; (3) the rapid expansion of other relatively new industries such as electric power, electrical equipment, radio and telephone, air transportation, motion pictures, and rayon; (4) the rapid pace of technological change, leading to great increases in labor productivity; and (5) the rise to a peak of a long building cycle. Superimposed on these was a wave of optimism that must in part be treated as an independent factor, a fairly high propensity to consume and an elastic credit supply.

It is impossible to say precisely how important the war was in creating a demand for plant and equipment. It is clear, however, that the pent-up demands that existed after the armistice were not satisfied during 1919–1920, and a substantial amount of investment in the early 1920's must have represented replacement and expansion programs deferred from the war years and investment to capitalize on technological changes occurring during the war.

The most important stimulus to investment and to expansion of total output in the 1920's was the automobile. Like electric power, this was a prewar innovation. But its full impact on the American economy was not felt until the 1920's. Production of motor vehicles had already risen from 485,000 in 1913 to 1,934,000 in 1919. Production jumped to 4,180,000 by 1923 and then rose further to a peak of 5,622,000 in 1929.

The effect of the automobile on aggregate demand came from two sources — the expansion in the *production* of cars and trucks and the enormously increased *use* of motor vehicles. The increase in production created a demand for new plant and equipment in both the automobile industry and the industries that served it: parts and accessories, rubber, steel, plate glass, lead, etc. These auxiliary industries were able, as automobile production grew, to expand their own production and employment and to invest in new plant and equipment.

Even more important was the growing *use* of automobiles. Motor vehicle production nearly trebled between 1919 and 1919, but the increase in registrations — the number of cars and trucks on the road — was even larger. And steadily greater use was made of each vehicle. The result was an enormous expansion in employment in oil refining, filling stations and garages, truck and bus driving, selling of supplies and accessories, and con-

struction and repair of roads. Expansion in these activities meant new investment — in buildings, equipment, and roads. And as the automobile changed methods of living, still further investment was required — in the development of suburban communities, for example.

Another prewar innovation, electric power, was a highly important stimulus to investment. Electric power production more than doubled between 1920 and 1929, and generating capacity increased in proportion. Use of this power in turn required electrical equipment and opened up methods of reducing costs that involved other types of new machinery. Value added by the electrical machinery industry also more than doubled between 1919 and 1929, compared to an increase of about 30 percent for manufacturing as a whole. Along with the growth of electric power production and the use of electrically driven machinery and handling equipment in industry went rapid expansion in the telephone industry (again a prewar innovation), the growth of radio (entirely a postwar development), and the rapid electrification of the home.

Other new industries and products helped to maintain investment and expand production — various chemical products (particularly rayon), oil and rubber products other than gasoline and tires, natural gas, production and distribution of motion pictures, the airplane, and so on. Most of these represented prewar innovations that added more to output in the postwar than in the prewar period.

Also highly important in stimulating investment was the increased tempo of technological change in the 1920's. Productivity per man-hour in manufacturing rose some 70 percent between 1919 and 1929. Mass production techniques were extended, greater use was made of automatic and special-purpose machinery, radical improvements occurred in material-handling methods, and so on. These developments made a major contribution to the demand for producers' durable goods. Labor costs fell steadily during the 1920's, as wages failed to rise as rapidly as productivity increased. As a result, stable or falling prices went together with expanded profit margins. The latter bolstered expectations and encouraged further investment; the former led to illusions, in the midst of the speculative boom for the late 1920's, that "conditions were fundamentally sound" because commodity prices were not rising.

As would be expected, corporate profits were high during most of the 1920's, though some industries (e.g., textiles) made a less profitable showing than others. Profit per unit in manufacturing was stable at a high level during 1923–1926, declined in 1927, and rose above the 1923–1926 level in 1929. The rate of profit on invested capital of manufacturing corporations remained at a high level, with no marked trend either upward or downward, between 1923 and 1929.

[It] has already [been] indicated how important construction was in maintaining investment in the 1920's. . . . The most important single component of new construction was residential building, which comprised 40 percent or more of the total through 1926, when a decline set in which lasted until 1933. In the nonresidential field, public-utility, government, and "other" construction (i.e., stores, office buildings, etc.) were all more important than strictly industrial (i.e., factory) building. About half the government figure represented road building. Some of the large volume of

building represented accumulated demand from the war years and the needs of an expanding population; part was in response to speculative enthusiasm and the ease with which mortgage credit could be obtained; part was the direct result of the automobile and the changes in living habits that it inspired. The large volume of commercial building reflected the great expansion in the trade, service, and finance industries that occurred during the 1920's. Only a minor part of total construction was required by expanding industrial production. . . .

* * *

The stock-market crash came in October, but most observers put the turning point in business several months earlier. The National Bureau's date is August, and the peak in the index of industrial production came at about the same time. Some other indicators turned down even earlier. Retail sales, however, did not decline until the last quarter of the year. We may view the period from about March to October as representing the "turning point zone" or critical period, within which the forces making for deflation gradually came into ascendancy.

It is impossible to give a complete and precise statement of the immediate causes of the downturn. Certainly the full explanation of the extent and severity of the Great Depression is not to be found merely in the sequence of events during 1928–1929; we must look at the boom of the 1920's as a whole and at the course of developments during 1930–1933.

* * *

We are now ready to try to summarize the cause of the Great Depression. Two questions need to be answered. First, what were the factors immediately responsible for the downturn in 1929? Second, how do we account for the length and severity of the downswing that followed? The second question is related to a third, dealing with the cycle of 1933–1938: What caused the recovery in the United States after 1933 to be so weak and halting and to stop so far short of full employment?

The immediate causes of the 1929 turning point have already been suggested and may be summarized as follows:

1. There was a weakening of short-term expectations associated with (a) the development of buyers' markets in particular lines (horizontal maladjustments) and (b) concern over the stock-market boom. Oversupply in the automobile industry was particularly important in this connection.
2. Deflationary pressure accumulated as a result of the decline in residential building which had been going on since early 1928. This was offset only as other forms of investment were increasing.
3. Most important, the abnormally high level of investment in 1928–1929 — on top of the substantial investment in the several preceding years — was beginning to create conditions of overcapacity in particular industries. This was one of the causes of the weakening of short-term expectations previously mentioned, but, more important, it led to a change in long-term expectations.
4. The developments mentioned were sufficient to begin the downswing. Then in October the stock-market crash provided the *coup de grâce* — depressing expectations, removing a cheap source of long-term capital, and reducing consumers' demand for luxuries and durable goods.

The international factors — the cessation of international lending and the pressure of supply on the prices of important primary products — were, in a sense, an independent set of causes operating chiefly on other countries, at least so far as the immediate causes of the downturn are concerned. They were not important in bringing the boom in the United States to an end.

The situation in 1929 was quite different from that prevailing at the time of the earlier downturns in the 1920's. Whereas in 1921, 1924, and 1927 the maladjustments could be corrected by a brief curtailment of output and liquidation of inventories, in 1929 businessmen came to doubt the profitability of continuing to invest in new plant and equipment at the rate such investment was being made in 1928 and the first half of 1929. Speculative optimism and technology had inspired in the middle and late 1920's a rate of investment in particular lines that could not be indefinitely maintained, and the acceleration of investment expenditures in 1928–1929 aggravated this tendency. Unlike the earlier downturns in the 1920's, a downward shift in short-term expectations in 1929 involved also a fundamental change in long-term expectations.

It is more accurate to say that the downturn in 1929 was due primarily to "overinvestment" than to ascribe the difficulty to "underconsumption." True, overinvestment was in relation to the demand for final products. But it is difficult to conceive of any increase in *total* consumption that would have maintained investment in a number of areas at the rate that had been reached before the turning point. It is true that wages did not rise as rapidly as productivity and that the propensity to consume apparently fell somewhat in 1929; but it can scarcely be argued that a moderately higher level of consumption could have prevented for very long, if at all, a decline in investment in residential and commercial building, in the automobile and related industries, and in other areas that had been expanding most rapidly. There was overinvestment in the late 1920's in the sense that capacity in numerous lines had been expanding at a rate that could not be indefinitely maintained.

The chief immediate cause of the downturn, then, was probably the impact of "partial overinvestment" on business expectations. This, however, is not sufficient to account for the length or severity of the depression or for its international ramifications. What we have said in earlier sections suggests that the following factors were chiefly responsible for the magnitude of the catastrophe that occurred.

1. The exhaustion of investment opportunities resulting from (a) the working of the acceleration principle in industries approaching maturity and (b) the creation of considerable excess capacity, particularly in residential and commercial building.
2. The financial excesses of the 1920's, which at the same time led to too rapid a rate of real investment in some industries and created a superstructure of inflated capital values the collapse of which weakened the banking system and led both borrowers and lenders to take a pessimistic view of the feasibility of further investment.
3. The unwise lending policies of the commercial banks, which created "frozen assets" on such a scale as to undermine the public's confidence in the entire banking system.
4. International balance-of-payments difficulties arising out of (a) the decline in American foreign lending, (b) the erratic movement of short-term capital, and (3) the serious oversupply situation in world primary markets, including some of the principal products of American agriculture.

It was these weaknesses, particularly the last three, that continued and deepened the downswing from 1931 on. The combination of these factors made the depression more severe than the other "major depressions" that we have had since the Civil War.

There remains the question: Why was the recovery of the 1930's so slow and halting in the United States, and why did it stop so far short of full employment? We have seen that the trouble lay with the inducement to invest. Even with abnormally low interest rates, the economy was unable to generate a volume of investment high enough, given the propensity to consume, to raise aggregate demand to the full-employment level. What made the general propensity to invest so low is a question that is still being vigorously debated.

One answer points to the reform measures of the Roosevelt administration. We have already expressed our own view that New Deal policies cannot be held completely responsible, though they undoubtedly did have a restrictive effect on long-term business expectations. There is no reason to believe that different government measures would have restored residential or commercial construction to the inflated levels of the 1920's, and the federal government can scarcely be blamed for the flattening out of growth curves in particular industries or for the "once-burned-twice-shy" attitude created in many investors' minds by the financial collapse after 1929. But we may grant, without further analysis, that willingness to invest in long-term projects was impaired to some but an unknown extent by the way business reacted to the activities of the federal government during these years. Needless to say, this conclusion carries no implications regarding the social desirability, from one or another point of view, of the measures that were taken.

Although much work remains to be done on the interwar period before we can evaluate with reasonable accuracy the importance of the different influences operating on business incentives in the 1930's, this writer is at present inclined to believe that government policies were not the most important factor holding back investment in those years. There seems to have been a lack of underlying investment opportunities, apart from the depressing effects of government actions and attitudes.

One group of writers holds that a fundamental change in the character of the American economy had occurred by the 1930's, with the result that the level of investment could be expected to be normally deficient in the future, given the existing propensity to consume. According to Hansen, the leading adherent of this view, rapid population growth and the opening up of new territory in various parts of the world were responsible for perhaps half of the total net investment in the nineteenth century. Technology was responsible for the remainder. In the 1930's, according to this view, we began to see the effect of the decline in population growth and in territorial expansion. Technology alone could not be expected to generate as high a rate of investment as all three stimuli working together; and in the 1930's even technol-

ogy did not provide as strong a stimulus as it did in earlier decades, when the railroad or the automobile and electric power were expanding most rapidly. Thus, in the 1930's the American economy was suffering from "secular stagnation" or "economic maturity" — a drying up of private investment opportunities. If the argument is granted, the solution is obvious. If aggregate demand is equal to the sum of $C + I + G$,[1] and if I remains too low for full employment, the answer lies in increased government spending or measures to raise the propensity to consume (or both).

This is not the place to attempt a critical valuation of the secular-stagnation thesis, which has attracted much less attention in the inflationary years following World War II than it did in the 1930's. There is unquestionably an important element of truth in the argument — particularly that part of it which stresses the effect of a declining rate of population growth on the opportunities for investment — for example, in residential building and in the further expansion of old industries. Even if technology prevents a secular decline in the level of investment, "underemployment equilibrium" may still be a danger. For as technology raises the full-employment level of real income, it is not sufficient that the level of investment remain constant. The volume of investment must rise to absorb an increased flow of saving. Else the propensity to consumer must increase or government spending must absorb the increased savings not absorbed by an expansion in private investment.

While "underemployment equilibrium" may be a future danger, there are difficuties in accepting the secular-stagnation

[1] In the equation, C, I, and G stand for spending by consumers, investors, and government, respectively. [Editor's note.]

thesis as an explanation of the disappointing behavior of investment in the 1930's. First of all, looking to the future as well as the past, the development of new industries and the expansion of old ones *may* still provide the necessary investment incentives, particularly if prices can be adjusted to achieve the maximum stimulation of demand. So far as the 1930's are concerned, the secular-stagnation argument is weak because it deals with secular — i.e., gradually operating — forces. Less than a decade separated 1928–1929 and 1936–1937, scarcely enough time for long-run forces to create the differences that existed between the periods. It is not sufficient to reply that secular stagnation was also operating in the 1920's but was temporarily offset by a speculative boom and by the investment opportunities created by the spread of the automobile and electric power.

Our own view is that stagnation existed in the 1930's, but that it did not necessarily have secular significance. Investment opportunities were restricted then because they had been so thoroughly exploited in the 1920's and because the severity of the financial liquidation after 1929 led businessmen and investors to view with a jaundiced eye the opportunities that were available. We would add that, given such a situation, the relative inflexibility of some prices (for example, building costs) prevented investment from being as high as it might otherwise have been. And, as noted before, the reaction of business to New Deal policies made the situation still worse.

By the end of the 1930's a good deal of excess capacity had been liquidated; residential construction was showing encouraging signs of revival; and technology was creating new investment opportunities. Had the war not intervened, private investment might or might not have increased to the point where full employment would have been possible without major government intervention. We shall never know, of course. The next decade or so, if the world can remain at peace, may throw additional light on the subject. In the years since World War II, the combination of private investment and a high level of government expenditures has been sufficient to give us sustained prosperity interrupted by only very mild recessions — although, as we noted in an earlier chapter, the rate of growth through most of the 1950's was somewhat disappointing and the level of unemployment did not fall below 4 percent in the latter half of the decade.

Suggestions for Additional Reading

Three notable and useful economic histories which describe the Great Depression and discuss its causes are Douglass North, *Growth and Welfare in the American Past: A New Economic History* (Englewood Cliffs, N. J., 1966); Thomas C. Cochran, *The American Business System: A Historical Perspective, 1900–1955* (New York, 1962); and Broadus Mitchell, *Depression Decade: From New Era through New Deal, 1929–1941* (New York, 1947).

Among the more significant of the analytical-descriptive works on the depression written by economists during the 1930's (in addition to those cited in the foregoing text) are: Lionel Robbins, *The Great Depression* (New York, 1936); Sumner Schlichter, "The Period 1919–1936 in the United States: Its Significance for Business Cycle Theory," *Review of Economic Statistics*, XIX, 1 (February 1937); H. V. Hodson, *Slump and Recovery, 1929–1932: A Survey of World Economic Affairs* (New York and London, 1938); the Brookings Institution study, *The Recovery Problem in the United States* (Washington, 1936); and the U. S. National Resources Committee's *Toward Full Use of Resources*, which is Part Two of its *Structure of the American Economy* (Washington, 1940).

Most of the postwar writing which economists have produced on the problem of economic fluctuations is either theoretical and generalized or directed to analysis of the contemporary economy. Rarely is attention focused on a concrete historical problem like the Great Depression, but there are a number of helpful works in addition to those previously cited in the text. For example, Gilbert Burck and Charles E. Silbern, "What Caused the Great Depression," and "Why the Depression Lasted So Long," both available conveniently in Richard Mulcahy (ed.), *Readings in Economics from Fortune* (New York, 1957), 82–88, 88–94, give a nontechnical treatment which takes account of contemporary economic thought. Also usable by the noneconomist are the following works, all of which deal entirely or to a considerable extent with interpreting economic events of the 1930's in the United States: Thomas Wilson, *Fluctuations in Income and Employment* (New York, 1948); Lawrence R. Klein, *Economic Fluctuations in the United States* (New York, 1950); George Terborgh, *The Bogy of Economic Maturity* (Chicago, 1945); M. D. Brockie, "Theories of the 1937–38 Crisis and Depression," *Economic Journal*, LX, 238 (June 1950); H. G. Fisher, "Hicks' 'Elementary Case' Economic Model for the United States, 1929–1941," *Journal of the American Statistical Association* (September 1952); "Is Another Major Contraction Likely?," *American Economic Review, Proceedings*, XLVIII, 2 (May 1958) (two papers by A. Achinstein and B. G. Hickman, with discussion by V. L. Bassie, E. P. Schmidt, and Daniel Hamberg); Kenneth D. Roose, "The Recession of 1937–38," *Journal of Political Economy*, LVI, 3 (June 1948); and I. O. Scott, Jr., "A Comparison of Production During the Depressions of 1873 and 1929," *American Economic Review*, XLII, 4 (September 1952).

Very illuminating for the depression in Britain and, by implication, for the United States, too, is H. W. Richardson, "The Basis of Economic Recovery in the 1930's: A Review and a New Interpretation," *Economic History Review*, II, 15 (December 1962). Also very rewarding as a basis for contrast and comparison is the key work by Ingvar Svennilson, *Growth and Stagnation in the European Economy* (Geneva, 1954).